JavaScript

Brian Jenkins

JavaScript

Programming

A Step-by-Step Guide for Absolute Beginners

Brian Jenkins

Book Objectives

The following are the objectives of this book:

- To help you know how to get started with JavaScript programming.

- To help you understand the syntax and constructs that make up the JavaScript scripting language.

- To help you transition from a JavaScript Beginner to a Professional.

- To help you understand how to use JavaScript to improve the interactivity of your website applications.

Who this Book is for?

The author targets the following groups of people:

- Anybody who is a complete beginner to JavaScript programming or computer programming in general.

- Anybody in need of advancing their JavaScript programming skills.

- Professors, lecturers or tutors who are looking to find better ways to explain JavaScript to their students in the simplest and easiest way.

- Students and academicians, especially those focusing on computer programming and web development.

What do you need for this Book?

Make sure that you have the following:

- A text editor such as notepad.

- A modern web browser.

What is inside the book?

The book has been grouped into chapters, with each chapter exploring a different feature of the JavaScript scripting language. The author has provided JavaScript codes, each code performing a different task. Corresponding explanations have also been provided alongside each piece of code to help the reader understand the meaning of the various lines of the code. In addition to this, screenshots showing the output that each code should return have been given. The author has used a simple language to make it easy even for absolute beginners to understand.

About the Author

Brian Jenkins has a Ph.D. in computer science. He conducted coding research for magnetic recording systems and long-haul fiber optic communication systems. With two decades of experience teaching programming to newcomers, and one of the most talented IT specialists of his generation, Dr. Brian works as a Research Software Specialist and occasional as a bioinformatician.

Since 2015 Brian lives in Geneva, with his wife, and daughter. He is working on a series of books on computer programming and data science.

"JavaScript is a language with more than its share of bad parts."

Douglas Crockford

Introduction

JavaScript is a powerful scripting language that every web developer should be familiar with. JavaScript has brought in many changes to the web development field. It has provided web developers with a way of making web pages more interactive. This is something most web visitors look for. If you know of validations, like checking whether a user enters correct details when filling forms, JavaScript is the best language to use for the implementation of such. It is one of the technologies of the WWW (World Wide Web). The good think with JavaScript is that it is supported by all modern web browsers. This means that you are not expected to get any special plugins to be able to run its scripts.

You can easily get started with writing and running JavaScript scripts because you only need basic elements like a text editor and a browser. Modern browsers come with the JavaScript Engine embedded; hence you don't need any other plugin to be able to run your scripts. The language also comes with many features and paradigms which you can rely on when writing your scripts. This book is an excellent guide for you on JavaScript programming. The author has discussed everything about JavaScript in a detailed manner. Enjoy reading!

To my wife and my daughter, you are the happiness of my days, and you are my truest love!

Contents

Chapter 6- JavaScript Loops

Chapter 7- JavaScript Functions

Chapter 8: JavaScript Objects

Chapter 15- Multimedia

Chapter 16- Error Handling

Chapter 17- Regular Expressions

Chapter 18- Image Map

Chapter 19- Page Redirection

Conclusion

Chapter 1- JavaScript Basics

What is JavaScript?

HTML was developed for content, **CSS** for presentation, but **JavaScript** was developed for interactivity. Originally, JavaScript was developed to add interactivity (such as animations and hovers) to small web pages, but it can now be used for nearly everything including large applications, games, and servers.

JavaScript programs are known as ***scripts***. You can write JavaScript inside the HTML of a web page and it will be executed automated when the page is being loaded. The scripts are provided in plain text and executed as they are. They don't require a compilation or a special preparation so as to run. Today, we can execute JavaScript code on a browser, server or on a device with a ***JavaScript Engine***. Initially, JavaScript was referred to as *LiveScript* because it made web pages alive. This name was later changed to JavaScript.

JavaScript is an object-based scripting language which can be interpreted by all modern-day browsers. This means that all browsers come with the JavaScript Engine. This has increased the popularity of JavaScript, making it the most popular scripting language today.

Environment Setup

To write, test and run your JavaScript code, you need the following:

- **Editor**
- **Browser**

You can write your JavaScript code using even a basic text editor such as Notepad. However, it is good for you to get an advanced text editor that will provide you with features such as syntax error highlighting, auto-completion, etc. Examples of such text editors include Visual Studio, Eclipse, Aptana, etc. These can help you with speedy development.

There are also online JavaScript editors that you can use for writing your scripts. A good example of this is jsfiddle.net.

For the case of the browser, you can install any type of browser depending on your preference. Examples of such browsers include Chrome, Internet Explorer, Safari, Firefox, Opera, etc. JavaScript can work on any browser running on any OS.

JavaScript Example

There are three places where we can place our JavaScript code. We can place the code within the body, within the head tag or in an external JavaScript file. Here is our first JavaScript example:

```
<script type="text/javascript">
document.write("JavaScript makes web pages
interactive!");
</script>
```

The code should print the following:

JavaScript makes web pages interactive!

The **script** tag has specified that we are using JavaScript. This will help the browser know the kind of data it has been provided with. The code simply calls the JavaScript's **document.write()** method which prints the text we pass to it. This method is used for displaying dynamic content using JavaScript.

As we have stated above, there are three places we can add our JavaScript code. The following code demonstrates how to add the code between the <body> and </body> tags:

```
<html>
<body>
<script type="text/javascript">
```

```
document.write("JavaScript makes web pages
interactive!");
</script>
</body>
</html>
```

Here is another example showing how we can show an alert box:

```
<html>
<body>
<script type="text/javascript">
 alert("Hello World");
</script>
</body>
</html>
```

We have called the **alert()** method which shows an alert box with the specified message. In this case, the message will be **Hello World**.

The JavaScript code can also be added within the **<head>** and **</head>** tags.

Here is an example:

```
<html>
<head>
<script type="text/javascript">
function hello(){
```

```
 alert("Hello World");
}
</script>
</head>
<body>
<p>JavaScript</p>
<form>
<input type="button" value="Click Me"
onclick="hello()"/>
</form>
</body>
</html>
```

We have created a method named **hello()** within the script tag. This method should return an alert box with the message **Hello World** when called. We have created a form with a button within the **<body> </body>** tags. The **onclick** property specifies the method to call when the button is clicked. After running the code, you should get the following:

JavaScript

Click Me

Click the **"Click Me"** button. You will see the alert box with the *Hello World* message.

That is how JavaScript code can be added within the **\<head\>** **\</head\>** tags.

We can also create an external JavaScript file then embed it into a number of web pages. Due to the ability to use such a page on many HTML pages, we can achieve code reusability.

Any external JavaScript file must be given a name that ends with a .js extension to mark it as a JavaScript file. All JavaScript code should be embedded into a single file to make the web page respond faster.

Let us create our external JavaScript file to return **Hello World** message within an alert box. The file will be given the name **hello.js**.

```
hello.js:
function hello(){
  alert("Hello World");
}
```

We can now create our HTML file and add the name of the JavaScript file to it. Here is the code for the html file:

```
index.html:
<html>
<head>
<script type="text/javascript"
src="hello.js"></script>
```

```
</head>
<body>
<p>JavaScript</p>
<form>
<input type="button" value="Click Me"
onclick="hello()"/>
</form>
</body>
</html>
```

The name of the JavaScript file was specified within the script tag using the *src* parameter.

JavaScript Comments

Comments provide us with a way of delivering messages. Comments help in guiding users, adding information describing the code, suggestions or warnings, making it easy for the reader to interpret code. The JavaScript Engine ignores comments, meaning that it just skips them.

JavaScript comments can span a single or multiple lines. To write a single-line comment, precede it with a double slash (**//**). For example:

```
<script>
// A single line comment in JavaScript
```

```
document.write("Hello World");
</script>
```

Here is another example:

```
var x=5;
var y=15;
var z=x+y;//To add values of x and y
document.write(z);//to print sum of 5 and 15
```

Multi-line comments are enclosed between /* and */ (a slash and an asterisk). This can also be used for a single line comment. For example:

```
<script>
/* A multi-line comment in JavaScript
The JavaScript engine will skip it */
document.write("Hello World");
</script>
```

Case Sensitivity

JavaScript is a case sensitive scripting language. This means that a variable the name *x* will be different from the variable named **X**. A variable named ***age*** will be different from the variables named ***Age***, ***AGE*** etc.

Chapter 2- Popup Message

JavaScript has numerous built-in methods that can help in displaying popup messages for various purposes. Let us discuss the various popup boxes provided by JavaScript:

Alert Box

This is used to show a message to a user, particular where the emphasis is needed. It comes with an **OK** button that closes the popup when clicked. It is created by calling the JavaScript's *alert()* function.

For example:

```
<html>
<body>
    <h1>Popup</h1>
        <script>
        alert("Hello World!");  // to display a
string message
        alert(12); // to display a number
        alert(true); // to display a boolean
    </script>
</body>
</html>
```

When you run the code, it will display the first alert box with the string **Hello World!** Click **OK** button and it will display an alert with **12**. Again, click the **OK** button and it will display an alert box with **true**. This shows that the alert box can be used to display a message of any type.

Confirm Box

Sometimes, a user is expected to give a confirmation so as to proceed. For example, you may want a user to confirm deletion or update of certain details before the process can be completed. This can be done using the **confirm()** function provided by JavaScript. This function will display a popup box to the user with two buttons namely **OK** and **Cancel**. The next step is determined by the button that the user clicks.

For example:

```
<html>
<body>
    <h1>confirm()</h1>
    <p id="del"></p>
    <script>
        var userChoice;
        if (confirm("Do you really want to
delete the data?") == true) {
```

```
            userChoice = "Data deleted
successfully!";
        } else {
            userChoice = "Delete Canceled!";
        }
    document.getElementById("del").innerHTML =
userChoice;
    </script>
</body>
</html>
```

Prompt Box

In some cases, you may need to receive an input from users and use it to perform further actions on the web page. For example, you may need to calculate the monthly amount for loan repayment based on the number of months within which the user wants to settle the loan. In such a case, you can use the *prompt()* function provided by JavaScript.

The function should take two string parameters. The first one is the message that will be displayed while the second one is the default value to be in the input text once the message has been displayed:

```
prompt([string display_message], [string
default_Value]);
```

For example:

```
<html>
<body>
    <h1>prompt()</h1>
    <p id="pro"></p>

    <script>
        var age = prompt("What is your age?",
"26");
    document.getElementById("pro").innerHTML =
"You are " + age + " years old";
    </script>
</body>
</html>
```

The code prompts you to enter your age. If you don't and click the **OK** button, **26** will be used as your default age.

Chapter 3- JavaScript Variables

A variable is a name for a storage location. From its name, it can vary. Variables hold values that can vary. In JavaScript, we use the *var* keyword to declare variables. Each variable must be given a unique name. You are allowed to assign a value to a variable during the time of its declaration. This can be done using the equals to symbol **(=)**.

The following is the syntax for declaring and initializing variables in JavaScript:

```
var variable-name;
var variable-name = value;
```

Here are valid examples of this:

```
var x = 1; // variable storing a numeric value
var y = 'nicholas';  // variable storing a
string value
var z;  // declare a variable and not assign a
value
```

We have used the *var* keyword to declare three variables. Two of the variables have been assigned a value. Note that this has been done at the time of their declaration.

We can also declare more than one variable in a single line and separate them by a comma **(,)**. This is demonstrated below:

```
var x = 1, y = 'nicholas', z;
```

Note that in JavaScript, one can declare a variable without using the ***var*** keyword. However, if you do this, ensure that you assign a value to the variable immediately. This is demonstrated below:

```
x = 1;
```

```
y = 'nicholas';
```

However, I don't recommend that you declare any variable without the use of ***var*** keyword. This is because you may end up overriding a global variable without knowing.

If a variable is declared without the ***var*** keyword, it automatically becomes a global variable, regardless of where it has been declared.

Here are the rules that govern the declaration of variable names in JavaScript:

1. The variable name should begin with an underscore **(_)**, a letter (either **A** to **Z** or **a** to **z**), or the dollar sign **($)**.
2. After the first letter, one can use digits in the variable name.
3. JavaScript variable names are case sensitive, example, p is different from P.

The following example demonstrates how to use variables in JavaScript:

```
<script>
var a = 12;
var b = 11;
var c= a + b;
document.write(c);
</script>
```

The code will return the sum of the two variable values, which is **23**.

Local Variables

These are variables that are defined within a block or a function. It can only be accessed from within the block or function within which it has been defined.

Here is an example:

```
<script>
function xyz(){
var a=12; // a local variable
}
</script>
```

The variable *a* can only be accessed from within the function *xyz()*.

Here is another example of local variable declaration:

```
<script>
If(5 < 10){
var a = 12; //a JavaScript local variable
}
</script>
```

The variable *a* in the above example can only be accessed from within the block of its declaration.

Global Variables

These are variables that can be accessed from any function. A global variable is usually declared outside a function or with the JavaScript's window object.

For example:

```
<script>
var val=12; //a global variable
function x(){
document.writeln(val);
}
function y(){
document.writeln(val);
}
x(); //calling a JavaScript function
y(); //calling a JavaScript function
```

```
</script>
```

The code will return the following:

```
12 12
```

The code demonstrates that the function can be referenced from different functions and its value will remain the same.

If you need to declare a global variable within a function, you must use the **window** object. For example:

```
window.val=12;
```

Such a variable can be declared within any function and accessed from any function.

For example:

```
<script>
function xy(){
window.val=12; //declaring a global variable
using window object
}
function xz(){
alert(window.val); //accessing a global variable
from another function
}
xy();
```

```
xz();
</script>
```

We have declared the variable **val** within the function **xy()** and assigned it a value of **12**. We have then accessed the same variable from the function **xz()**. This returns a value of **12**.

After declaring a variable outside a function, it is internally added to the **window** object. The object can at the same time be accessed via the **window** object.

Here is an example:

```
<script>
var val = 12;
function xy(){
alert(window.val); //accessing a global variable
}
</script>
```

Each programming language supports a number of data types. They represent the types of values which can be represented then manipulated in the programming language. JavaScript supports **3** primitive data types including:

1. Numbers such as **1, 8, 90, 345** etc.
2. Strings, which are texts, for example, **"My name"** etc.
3. Boolean, which can be true or false?

JavaScript is also capable of supporting **2** trivial data types, namely **null** and **undefined**. It also has a composite data type called **object**.

Note that in JavaScript, there is no difference between integers and floats. In JavaScript, all numbers are represented in the form of floating-point values.

Comparing variables

In JavaScript, variables can be compared in different ways. We can compare whether two variables are equal or not by use of double equals sign.

Example:

```
<script>
x=30;
y=30;
  if (x==y) {
alert("x equals y")
};
  </script>
```

When executed, the script will show a pop up with the text **"x equals y"** as shown below:

This is the values of the two values are equal, that is, **10**. If not, nothing will happen once the script is executed.

Other than numbers, we can also compare strings as shown below:

```
<script>
firstname="Nicholas";
lastname="Samuel";
 if (lastname=="Samuel") {alert("Correct
name!")};
</script>
```

The comparison will evaluate to a true, so you will get a popup with the text **"Correct name!"** as shown below:

Correct name!

OK

Note that when doing a comparison, we use double equals sign (==). If you instead use a single equal' sign, the value on the right side of the sign will become the value of value (variable) on left side. An example is given below:

```
if (lastname="Samuel") {alert("Correct name!")};
```

Chapter 4- JavaScript Operators

JavaScript supports the use of operators. An operator performs an operation on one or many operands to produce a result. For example:

 + 3

In the above example, 2 and 3 are the operands while + is the operator. 2 is the left operand while 3 is the right operand. The + operator will add the two to give a result of 5. Let us discuss the various types of operators supported in JavaScript.

Logical Operators

These types of operators help us in connecting either one or more conditions. The following are the logical operators supported in JavaScript:

- **&&**- the **AND** operator. It checks whether the two operands are non-zero. If yes, it returns a **1**, otherwise, it returns a **0**.
- **||**- the **OR** operator. It checks whether any of the operands is non-zero. If yes, it returns a **1**, otherwise a **0**.
- **!**- the **NOT** operator. For reversing the Boolean result of an operand or condition.

For example:

```html
<html>
<body>
    <h1>Logical Operators</h1>
    <p id="pg1"></p>
    <p id="pg2"></p>
    <p id="pg3"></p>
    <p id="pg4"></p>
    <p id="pg5"></p>
    <script>
        var x = 12, y = 5;
    document.getElementById("pg1").innerHTML =
(x != y) && (x < y);
        document.getElementById("pg2").innerHTML
= (x > y) || (x == y);
        document.getElementById("pg3").innerHTML
= (x < y) || (x == y);
        document.getElementById("pg4").innerHTML
= !(x < y);
        document.getElementById("pg5").innerHTML
= !(x > y);
    </script>
</body>
</html>
```

The code prints the following result:

Logical Operators

false

true

false

true

false

In the above example, we have used the values of variables x and y to run various logical operators.

Arithmetic Operators

In JavaScript, you can perform arithmetic operations on your variables. These operations include addition (+), subtraction (-), multiplication (*), modulus (%), increment (++), decrement (--) etc. Example:

```
<script type="text/javascript">
a=1;
a=1; a++; //a=2
a=1; a--; //a=0
a=1; b=2; c=a+b; //c=3
a=1; d=a+4; //d=5
```

```
First="Edwin";
Last="Peter";
Name=First+" "+Last; //Name=Edwin Peter
a=3*7; //a=21
b=10/2; //b=5
c=(10/2)*2; //c=10
d=10/(1*2); //d=5
</script>
```

The results from the various lines have been shown in the comment section, that is, after //. The two forward slashes, that is, //, denote the beginning of a comment in JavaScript.

Assignment Operators

These are operators that help us assign values to variables. They include the following:

- = - to assign the right operand value to the left operand.
- += - to sum up the left and right operand values then assign the obtained result to left operand.
- -= - to subtract the right operand value from the left operand value then assign the obtained result to left operand.
- *= - to multiply the left and right operand values then assign the obtained result to left operand.

- /= - to divide the left operand value by the right operand value then assign the obtained result to left operand.
- %= - to get the modulus of the left operand divided by the right operand then assign the resulting modulus to left operand.

Here is an example:

```
<html>
<body>
    <h1> Assignment Operators</h1>

    <p id="pg1"></p>
    <p id="pg2"></p>
    <p id="pg3"></p>
    <p id="pg4"></p>
    <p id="pg5"></p>
    <p id="pg6"></p>
    <script>
        var a = 10, b = 20;
        a = b;
    document.getElementById("pg1").innerHTML =
a;
        a += 1;
    document.getElementById("pg2").innerHTML =
a;
```

```
        a -= 1;
    document.getElementById("pg3").innerHTML =
a;

        a *= 5;
    document.getElementById("pg4").innerHTML =
a;

        a /= 5;
    document.getElementById("pg5").innerHTML =
a;

        a %= 2;
    document.getElementById("pg6").innerHTML =
a;
    </script>
</body>
</html>
```

The code will return the following result:

20

21

20

100

20

0

The expression *a* = *b*; changed the value of variable *a* from **10** to **20**. That is why the first statement prints a **20**. We then begin to work with a value of a being **20**. The expression a += 1; increases the value of *a* by **1**, so it becomes **21**. This becomes the new value of variable *a*. The expression *a* -= *1*; subtracts a 1 from the current value of variable *a*, which is **21**, returning a **20**. This becomes the new value of variable *a*. The expression *a* *= *5*; multiplies the value of variable *a*, which is **20** by **5**, returning **100**. This becomes the new value of variable *a*. The expression *a* /= *5*; divides the value of variable a by **5**, returning **20**. This becomes the new value of variable a. The expression *a* %= *2*; returns the remainder after dividing the value of variable a by **2**, returning a **0**.

Chapter 5- JavaScript Decision Making

JavaScript comes with decision making statements that help in controlling the flow of programs. With these statements, the action taken is based on the condition met. JavaScript supports the following three decision making statements:

- **If Statement**
- **If else statement**
- **if else if statement**

If Statement

This statement should only be used when you need to take an action based on a certain condition. The content will only be evaluated if the condition is true. The statement takes the following syntax:

```
if(expression){
//the content to evaluate
}
```

For example:

```
<script>
        if( 10 < 5 )
        {
            alert("10 is less than 5");
```

```
        }

        if( 10 > 5)
        {
            alert("10 is greater than 5");
        }
    </script>
```

The code will return the following upon execution:

10 is greater than 5

OK

The first *if* condition evaluated to a *false*, hence its block of code was skipped. The second *if* condition evaluated to a *true*, hence its block of code was executed to give us the above output.

If...else Statement

This statement will evaluate the condition of whether the condition is true or false.

The statement has the following syntax:

```
if(condition)
{
    // code...
}
else{
    // code...
}
```

For example:

```
<script>
var x=100;
if(x%2==0){
document.write("x is an even number");
}
else{
document.write("x is an odd number");
}
</script>
```

In the above code, we are checking whether the value of variable x is an even number or not. The code returns the following:

x is an even number

The expression $x\%2==0$ checks the remainder after dividing **x** by **2**. If the remainder is 0, then x is an even number, otherwise, it is an odd number.

If...else if Statement

Sometimes, you may have multiple options on which you should make a decision. This statement helps us achieve this is JavaScript. The statement has the syntax given below:

```
if (expression_1){
    Statement(s)
}

else if (expression_2){
    Statement(s)
}

else if (expression_3){
    Statement(s)
}

else{
    Statement(s)
}
```

We only have a series of *if* statements which have been combined with the *else* statement. The statements to be executed are the one whose conditions evaluate to true.

For example:

```
<script>
var grade="B";
if(grade=="A"){
document.write("Excellent!");
}
else if(grade=="B"){
document.write("Good!");
}
else if(grade=="C"){
document.write("Fair");
}
else{
document.write("Poor!");
}
</script>
```

The value of grade is **B**. all the conditions will be matched and the *grade=="B"* condition will evaluate to a *true*. The code will return **"Good!"**.

Switch Statement

This statement helps us perform varied actions which depend on various conditions. It is suitable when you have many branches depending on the value of a single variable. With a switch statement, an expression evaluates various statements to be executed depending on the value of an expression.

The JavaScript interpreter must check every case against expression's value until it finds a match. If no match is found, then the default is chosen. Its syntax is as follows:

```
switch (expression) {
    case i:
        code
        break;
    case i:
        code
        break;
    default:
        code
}
For example:
<script>
var name ='Nicholas';
var output;
```

```javascript
switch(name){
case 'Samuel':
output = "Your name is Samuel";
break;
case 'Michelle':
output="Your name is Michelle";
break;
case 'Nicholas':
output = "Your name is Nicholas";
break;
default:
output = "No Name";
}
document.write(output);
</script>
```

The code will return the following upon execution:

Your name is Nicholas

Chapter 6- JavaScript Loops

Loops are good when you need to execute your code repeatedly, for a known or an unknown number of times. With loops, you can automate tasks that could have been tedious performing them manually. A good example is when you need to fill a table with values. You can use a loop to iterate through the cells of the tables while filling the values instead of filling them manually.

Let us discuss the various loop statements supported in JavaScript:

For Loop

This loop is used to iterate over a block of code for a fixed number of times. It is suitable when one is aware of the number of times to iterate over a block of code. The loop takes the following syntax:

```
for (initializer; condition; increment)
{
    // code
}
```

The *initializer* sets a counter variable that we should start with. The *condition* specifies criteria that must be met for the next iteration to be executed. The *increment* can either increment or decrement the counter.

Here is an example of a *for* loop:

```
<script>
for (x=0; x<5; x++)
{
document.write(x + "<br/>")
}
</script>
```

The variable *x* in the loop was first initialized to a value of **o**. The condition states that the value of variable *x* should be less than **5**. In the increment, the value of the variable *x* should be incremented by **1** after every iteration. This means that the loop should run from **o** to **4** to give the following result:

```
0
1
2
3
4
```

Here is another example:

```
<html>
<head>
<title>Length Converter</title>
</head>
```

```
<body>
<table border=4>
<tr><td>Length in Meters</td><td>Length in
Centimeters</td></tr>
<script language="javascript">
for (length=0; length<=20; length=length+2)
{
document.write("<tr><td>"+length+"</td><td>"
+(length * 100)+"</td></tr>");
}
</script>
</table>
</body>
</html>
```

We have used a *for* loop to iterate through a set of values while converting them from centimeters into meters. This time, we are incrementing the values by **2** rather than **1** after every iteration. The code returns a populated table as shown below:

Length in Meters	Length in Centimeters
0	0
2	200
4	400
6	600
8	800
10	1000
12	1200
14	1400
16	1600
18	1800
20	2000

While Loop

This loop can be used to iterate over code for an infinite number of times. It is suitable for use when one doesn't know the exact number of times to execute a loop. The loop will execute as long as the specified condition is true. Immediately the conditions become a *false*, the execution of the loop will halt. It takes the following syntax:

```
while (variable<=final_value)
{
// Script code.
}
```

For example:

```
<script>
var x=0;
while (x<=5)
{
document.write(x + "<br/>");
x++;
}
</script>
```

The *while* loop will run as long as the value of the variable *x* is not more than **5**.

The code returns the following:

```
0
1
2
3
4
5
```

Here is another example:

```
<html>
<head>
<title> Length Converter </title>
</head>
```

```
<body>
<table border=3>
<tr><td>Length in Meters</td><td>Length in
Centimeters</td></tr>
<script language="javascript">
length=0;
while (length<=20)
{
document.write("<tr><td>"+length+
"</td><td>"+(length * 100)+"</td></tr>");
length = length+2;
}
</script>
</table>
</body>
</html>
```

The above loop will always run as long as the value of *length* is less than or equal to **20**. Immediately the loop finds itself violating this condition, it will stop execution.

The code returns the following:

Length in Meters	Length in Centimeters
0	0
2	200
4	400
6	600
8	800
10	1000
12	1200
14	1400
16	1600
18	1800
20	2000

Do while Loop

This is a good loop for iterating a block of code for infinite number of times. However, the code must be executed once, regardless of the state of the condition, whether true or false. Its syntax is as follows:

```
do{
        statement (s)
}while (condition);
```

A *while* may never run, but the *do while* loop must run for at least once.

Here is an example:

```
<script>
var x= ;
do{
document.write(x + "<br/>");
x++;
}while (x<= );
</script>
```

The code will print the following result:

```
0
1
2
3
4
5
```

Loop Control Statements

We can control how loops are executed by use of *break* and *continue* statements. Sometimes, you may need to exit a loop before its end is reached. Also, you may also need to skip some part of a loop and execute the section which comes next. These two statements can help us achieve this.

Break Statement

With this statement, one can exit the loop early and get out of curly braces. Execution goes to the block after the loop.

Example:

```
<script type="text/javascript">
            var p = 1;
        document.write("Starting the loop<br />
");
            while (p < 20)
        {
          if (p == 5){
             break; // get out of loop
          }
          p = p + 1;
          document.write( p + "<br />");
        }
            document.write("Leaving the
loop<br /> ");
            </script>
```

That is how you can use a *break* statement in a *while* loop. The maximum value of *p* should be **20**. However, we have instructed the JavaScript interpreter to *break* once the value of *p* is **5**. The execution of the loop will stop at that point; the output should show numbers **2** to **5** as shown below:

```
Starting the loop
2
3
4
5
Leaving the loop
```

Continue Statement

With the ***continue*** statement, we can break our current loop, then proceed with the next value. Supposing you need to divide a certain number by numbers ranging between **-5** to **+5**. You need to skip division by 0 since it is illegal. This can be skipped using the ***continue*** statement. This can be implemented as follows:

```
<script type="text/javascript">
    for (p=-5; p<=5; p=p+1)
{
if (p==0) {continue};
document.write((10/p)+"<br>");
}
</script>
```

With such an implementation, the integer 10 will not be divided by 0.

The code will return the following result:

```
-2
-2.5
-3.3333333333333335
-5
-10
10
5
3.3333333333333335
2.5
2
```

We have skipped division by **0** as it will generate an error if we continued from **1**.

Chapter 7- JavaScript Functions

JavaScript functions are used for performing operations. Functions are a good way of grouping code together. Such code should be related in terms of the tasks they should perform. You only have to group the code together and assign it a unique name. From that point, you can call the code any number of times you want, facilitating code reuse.

With functions, you can enjoy the benefit of only having to do code rewriting or no rewriting at all.

Function Definition

The definition and call of a JavaScript function takes the following syntax:

```
// function definition
function <function_name>()
{
    // code to execute
};
//call the function
<function_name>();
```

As shown in the above syntax, the function is given a name which is used when calling the function to perform its intended task. The function has a body placed within curly braces (**{}**). The following is an example:

```
<html>
<body>
    <script>
        function HelloFunction() {
            document.write("Hello World");
        }
        HelloFunction();
    </script>
</body>
</html>
```

We have defined a function named ***HelloWorld ().*** Inside the body of the function, we have stated that the function should print the text ***Hello World***. Immediately after the body of the function, we have called it by its name. The code returns the following:

```
Hello World
```

Notice the method we have used to call the above function. The function will be called immediately the web page is loaded. However, many are the times we need to call functions by click of a button.

This is possible with JavaScript as demonstrated below:

```
<html>
<body>
<script>
function HelloFunction() {
 alert("Hello World");
}
</script>
<input type="button" onclick="HelloFunction()"
value="Hello"/>
</body>
</html>
```

We have used our previous function. However, we have created a button with the text **Hello** on it. The **onclick** property states what should happen after clicking the button. It states that after the button is clicked, the **HelloFunction()** function should be called. Run the code and click the Hello button. You will get the alert box with the necessary message:

Hello World

OK

Function Arguments

A function can take either one or more than one arguments, also known as **parameters**. The arguments should be supplied by calling code and they can be used inside the function. JavaScript is well known for being a dynamic scripting language, so the function argument can take an argument of any data type.

Consider the following example:

```
<script>
        function MyFunction(arg1, arg2) {
            alert("You passed " + arg1 + " and "
+ arg2);
        }

        MyFunction(10, 12);
        MyFunction("Nicholas", "Samuel");
        MyFunction("Nicholas", 26);
    </script>
```

We have created a function named **MyFunction** taking two arguments namely **arg1** and **arg2**. The function is to concatenate the values of these two arguments with a text and show them on an alert box. We have then called the same function three times, passing different parameters each time. After running the code, click the ok button to move through the sequence of alert boxes. The first dialog should be as follows:

You passed 10 and 12

OK

Note that the arguments will be passed to the function in the order that you specify them.

Here is another example:

```html
<html>
<body>
<script>
function calculateCube(x){
alert(x * x * x);
}
</script>
<form>
<input type="button" value="Calculate Cube"
onclick="calculateCube(3)"/>
</form>
</body>
</html>
```

We have created a button with the text **Calculate Cube** on it. When clicked, this button should call the ***calculateCube()*** function. In the ***onclick*** parameter, we have specified the function and passed an argument of **3** to it. This means that it should return the cube of **3**, which is **27**. Just run the program and click the **Calculate Cube** button.

Note that when calling a function, you can pass either more or fewer parameters. If you pass fewer parameters than the function expects, the rest will remain undefined. If you pass more arguments, the excess ones will be ignored. This is demonstrated in the following example:

```
<script>
        function MyFunction(arg1, arg2) {
            alert("You passed " + arg1 + " and "
+ arg2);
        }

        MyFunction(10, 12, 17);
        MyFunction("Nicholas", "Samuel");
        MyFunction("Nicholas");
    </script>
```

The Arguments Object

Any JavaScript function can use the arguments object. This object has a value for every parameter. It is similar to an array. Its values can be accessed using an index in the same way as an array. However, this object cannot support array methods.

Consider the following example:

```
<script>
        function MyFunction(arg1, arg2) {
            alert("You passed " + arguments[0] +
"  and " + arguments[1]);
        }

        MyFunction(10, 12, 17);
        MyFunction("Nicholas", "Samuel");
        MyFunction("Nicholas");
    </script>
```

The code will run as usual. When calling a function, we can pass arguments to it. The JavaScript interpreter treats the first arguments as being at index 0. The expression *arguments[0]* denotes the first argument when calling the function while the expression *arguments[1]* denotes the second argument when calling the function.

We can use a **for** loop to iterate over the arguments object. For example:

```
<script>
        function MyFunction() {
                for(var x = 0; x < arguments.length;
x++){
                        alert(arguments[x]);
                }
        }
        MyFunction("Nicholas", "Samuel");
    </script>
```

Two arguments have been passed to the function, and we have used the variable x within a *for* loop to iterate through these.

Return Value

In JavaScript, a function can use the **return** keyword to return either zero or one value.

Consider the example given below:

```
<script>
function MyFunction(){
return "Hello sir/madam";
}
```

```
</script>
<script>
document.write(MyFunction());
</script>
```

The function will return what has been specified in the statement with the **return** keyword.

Here is another example:

```
<html>
<body>
    <p id="pg1"></p>
    <p id="pg2"></p>
    <script>
        function Addition(x, y) {
            return x + y;
        };
        document.getElementById("pg1").innerHTML
= Addition(10,12);

        function Product(x, y) {
            console.log( x * y);
        };
    document.getElementById("pg2").innerHTML =
Product(10,12);
    </script>
```

```
</body>
</html>
```

The code will print the following:

```
22

undefined
```

We have created a function named *Addition()* that adds and returns the sum of two variables, x and y. The calling code is capable of getting the return value and assigns it to a variable. We also defined a second function named *Product()* which returns nothing, hence its result will be *undefined*.

In JavaScript, we can have a function returning another function. Here is an example of this:

```
<html>
<body>
    <p id="pg1"></p>
    <p id="pg2"></p>

    <script>
        function myfunction(a) {

            function product(b)
            {
```

```
                return a * b;
        }
        return product;
    }


    var db = myfunction( );
    document.getElementById("pg1").innerHTML
= db( );
    document.getElementById("pg2").innerHTML =
db( );
    </script>
</body>
</html>
```

The function named ***myfunction()*** is returning the function named ***product()***.

Function Expression

With JavaScript, we can assign a variable to our function and then use that variable as the function. This is given the name a ***function expression***.

For example:

```
<html>
<body>
```

```
<p id="pg1"></p>
<p id="pg2"></p>
<script>
    var sum = function Addition(x, y) {
        return x + y;
    };
document.getElementById("pg1").innerHTML =
sum(10, 12);
    document.getElementById("pg2").innerHTML =
Addition(10, 12); // invalid
    </script>
</body>
</html>
```

The code should return the sum of **10** and **12**, which is **22**. This output will be from the ***sum(10, 12)*** expression whereby we are calling the function using the variable we assigned to it. The expression ***Addition(10, 12)*** is not valid as we are calling the function by its name while it has already been assigned a variable.

Anonymous Function

In JavaScript, we can define a function without a name. Such a function is known as an ***anonymous function***. You must assign a variable to your anonymous function.

For example:

```
<script>
        var helloMessage = function (){
            alert("Hello World");
        };
        helloMessage();
        var message = function (name) {
            alert("Hi " + name);
        };
        helloMessage();
        message("Nicholas");
    </script>
```

We have created two anonymous functions. The first one takes no argument and it has been assigned the ***helloMessage*** variable. The message should return the ***Hello World*** message in an alert box. This method has been called twice in the program using the ***helloMessage();*** expression.

We have created the second anonymous function taking one argument that is, ***name***. This function has been assigned the variable named ***message***. We have called this method using this variable and passed the argument ***Nicholas*** to it. The code will show the ***Hello World*** message twice and the ***Hi Nicholas*** message once. To move from one alert box to another, click the **OK** button.

Hello World

OK

Nested Functions

JavaScript functions can have one or many inner functions. The nested functions should be within the score of the outer function. The inner function is allowed to access both the parameters and variables of the outer function. However, an outer function is not able to access the variables defined within its inner functions. Consider the following example:

```
<script>
        function OuterFunc(name)
        {
            function InnerFunc() {
                document.write("Hi " + name);
            }
            return InnerFunc();
        }
        OuterFunc("Nicholas");
```

```
</script>
```

We have defined an outer function named **OuterFunc()**. This function takes one parameter **name**. We have created an inner function named **InnerFunc()**. Although the **name** parameter belongs to the outer function, the inner function successfully accessed it. The code should print the following:

Hi Nicholas

Chapter 8: JavaScript Objects

Arrays

An object in JavaScript is an entity with both state and behavior. In JavaScript, everything is treated as an object. An array is an object which represents elements of a similar type. It has a fixed size, and its elements are stored sequentially. There are **3** ways of constructing arrays in JavaScript:

- **Array literal**
- **Array Instance**
- **Array constructor**

Array Literal

Creation of an array by use of array literal takes the following syntax:

```
var name_of_array=[val1,val2.....valN];
```

The values are added with square brackets **[]** and separated using commas.

Example:

```
<script type="text/javascript">
  var array1=["Nicholas","Samuel","Vickie"];
```

```
for (j=0;j<array1.length;j++){
document.write(array1[j] + "<br/>");
}
</script>
```

We have created the array **array1** with three values, which are names of individuals. A **for** loop has been used to iterate the values of the array, and then we have printed them. The **.length** property normally returns the array length. Once executed, the values in the array will be printed as shown below:

Nicholas
Samuel
Vickie

Creating an Array Directly

An array can be created directly by following the syntax given below:

```
var name_of_array=new Array();
```

With the **new** keyword, an instance of an array is created. Example:

```
    <script type="text/javascript">
var x;
var array2 = new Array();
```

```
array2[0] = "Nicholas";
array2[1] = "Samuel";
array2[2] = "Vickie";
for (x=0;x<array2.length;x++){
document.write(array2[x] + "<br>");
}
</script>
```

In the example, we have used the *new* keyword to create the array named *array2.* The next step is to populate elements in the array. Note that the position of array elements is denoted using indices. The first element in the array is at index **0**, the second element at index **1**, and the chain continues. Consider the following line:

```
array2[1] = "Samuel";
```

The line states that we store the element **"Samuel"** at index **1** of the array named *array2*. We have then used the variable *x* so as to iterate these elements of the array and print them.

Array Constructor

We create an instance of the array by simply passing arguments in the constructor instead of providing the value explicitly. The script given below demonstrates this:

```
<script type="text/javascript">
```

```
    var array3=new
Array("Nicholas","Samuel","Vickie");
    for (x=0;x<array3.length;x++){
    document.write(array3[x] + "<br>");
    }
```

</script>

In the above example, we have created an array named **array3**. The creation of the array and addition of elements to it has been done in the same line using a constructor. The **for** loop helps us iterate through the array elements and print them to the screen.

Array Methods

JavaScript comes with many in-built array methods that we can use to manipulate the elements of the array. Let us discuss these methods:

concat()

The **concat()** method combines arrays to return a single string. The arrays can be two or more. Note that the elements of the initial array will not be changed.

The methods take the following syntax:

```
array.concat(array1, array2,...., array_n)
```

the parameters to the method are the arrays that you need to concatenate. The method returns a new object which is a combination of all the arrays.

Consider the following example:

```
<script>
var array1=["Nicholas", "James", "Jane"];
var array2=["Alex", "Fidel", "Alice"];
var output=array1.concat(array2);
document.writeln(output);
</script>
```

We have created two arrays, *array1* and *array2*. Each array has a list of name. We have concatenated these two arrays into one object named *output*. The code will print the following output:

Nicholas.James.Jane.Alex.Fidel.Alice

In the above example, we have concatenated two arrays. A concatenation of three arrays can be obtained as follows:

```
<script>
var array1=["Nicholas", "James", "Jane"];
var array2=["Alex", "Fidel", "Alice"];
var array3=["Joel", "Mercy", "George"];
var output=array1.concat(array2,array3);
```

```
document.writeln(output);
</script>
```
The code will return the following result:

Nicholas.James.Jane.Alex.Fidel.Alice.Joel.Mercy.George

Other than creating different arrays and trying to concatenate the objects, we can concatenate the objects directly. This is demonstrated in the following example:

```
<script>
var array1=["Nicholas", "James", "Jane"];
var output=array1.concat("Alex", "Fidel",
"Alice");
document.writeln(output);
</script>
```
The code will return the following example:

Nicholas.James.Jane.Alex.Fidel.Alice

copyWithin()

When this method is used, it will copy a part of a given array with own elements and return the modified array. Note that the length of the modified array will not be changed.

The method takes the syntax given below:

```
array.copyWithin(target,start,end)
```

The **target** is where the copied element will take place. The **start** parameter is optional. It denotes the index from which copying of the elements by the method will begin. Its default value is 0, meaning that copying begins at index **0**, which is the first element of the array. The **end** parameter is also optional. It denotes the index at which the method will stop the copying process. It has a default value of **array.length-1**, which is the last element in the array.

The method returns a modified array. Consider the example given below:

```
<script>
var array1=["Nicholas", "James", "Jane",
"Alice", "George"];
// place at index 0, the element between 1st and
3rd elements
var output=array1.copyWithin(0,1,2);
document.writeln(output);
</script>
```

The code returns the following:

James.James.Jane.Alice.George

What has happened is that the element between the 1st and the 3rd elements was copied to the index 0. That is why the element **Nicholas** was replaced by the element **James.** The rest of the array elements have not been affected.

Let us see how we can provide only the target and start indexes:

```
<script>
var array1=["Nicholas", "James", "Jane",
"Alice"];
var output=array1.copyWithin(1,2);
document.writeln(output);
</script>
```

The code should return the following:

Nicholas.Jane.Alice.Alice

It is also possible for us to provide only the target index:

```
<script>
var array1=["Nicholas", "James", "Jane",
"Alice", "George"];
var output=array1.copyWithin();
document.writeln(output);
</script>
```

The code will return the following result:

Nicholas.James.Nicholas.James.Jane

fill()

This method is used for filling the elements of an array with some specified static values. When used, the original array is modified. If none of the elements has met the condition, this method will return undefined. It takes the following syntax:

```
array.fill(value[, start[, end]])
```

The **value** parameter denotes the static value that is to be filled. The **start** parameter is optional. It is the index from which filling will begin. Its default value is **0**, which is the first element in the array. The **end** parameter is also optional. It denotes the index at which filling of the values will stop. It returns a modified array.

Consider the following example:

```
<script>
var array1=["Nicholas", "James", "Jane",
"Alice", "George"];
var output=array1.fill("Joel");
document.writeln(array1);
</script>
```

The code will return the following:

Joel.Joel.Joel.Joel.Joel

All the array values have been replaced with Joel. Let us see how we can provide or state the starting index:

```
<script>
var array1=["Nicholas", "James", "Jane",
"Alice", "George"];
var output=array1.fill("Joel",2);
document.writeln(array1);
</script>
```

In the above example, the filling will start at the element after index 2. The code should return the following result:

Nicholas.James.Joel.Joel.Joel

The following example demonstrates how we can state both the start and the stop/end indexes:

```
<script>
var array1=["Nicholas", "James", "Jane",
"Alice", "George"];
var output=array1.fill("Joel",1,3);
document.writeln(array1);
</script>
```

The code should return the following:

Nicholas.Joel.Joel.Alice.George

every()

The purpose of this method is to check whether all the array elements satisfy the given condition. If all array elements meet the condition, the method will return a *true*, otherwise *false*. The method takes the syntax given below:

```
array.every(callback(current-value, index,
arr),thisArg)
```

The *callback* is the function for testing the condition. The *current-value* denotes the current element of the array. The *index* parameter is optional and it denotes the index of the current element. The *arr* parameter denotes the array to which we are to apply the *every()* function. The *thisArg* is an optional parameter. This is the value to be used as this during the execution of the callback. The method returns a *Boolean* value.

Consider the following example:

```
<script>
var marks=[20, 25, 15, 37, 27];
function confirm(x)
{
```

```
   return x>10;   //to return true as all marks
are above 10

}
document.writeln(marks.every(confirm));
</script>
```

The code returns **true**. We have defined an array with a set of integer values, which are marks. All marks are above **10**. The purpose of the **confirm()** is to check whether all marks are above **10**. Since this is true, the **every()** function returns a **true**. Let us change one of the values to be below **10** and see what happens:

```
<script>
var marks= [20, 5, 15, 37, 27];
function confirm(x)
{
   return x>10;   //to return true as all marks
are above 10

}
document.writeln(marks.every(confirm));
</script>
```

The code will return a **false** as the marks at index 1 is less than **10**, that is, **5**.

In the example given below, we are checking the number of elements present in the array:

```
<script>
function confirm(item, index, array) {
  return index < 3;
}
document.writeln([20, 5].every(confirm)); //true
document.writeln([20, 5, 1, 35,
46].every(confirm)); //false
</script>
```

The outputs are shown as comments. In the first execution of the method, we are passing an array with two elements, **20** and **5**. Our condition checks whether we have a total of **3** or fewer elements. Since we only have two elements, this will give us *true*. In the second case, our array has **5** elements. Since these are more than **3**, it will return a *false*.

find()

This method will return the first element in an array that meets the specified condition. It takes the following syntax:

```
array.find(callback(value,index,arr),thisArg)
```

The **callback** is the function that is to execute every element. The **value** is the current element of the array. The **index** parameter is optional. It denotes the index of the current element. The **arr** is also an optional parameter. It is the array that was operated by the **find()** method. The parameter **thisArg** is also optional. It denotes the value to be used as this during the execution of the callback.

The following example demonstrates how to use the **find()** method:

```
<script>
var array1=[20, 45, 14, 33, 18];
var output=array1.find(x=>x>20);
document.writeln(output)
</script>
```

In the above code, we are checking for an element whose value is greater than **20**. The method will first find **45**, hence this should be the output.

The following example demonstrates how we can use the same method to find a prime number:

```
<script>
function checkPrime(item, index, arr) {
  var start = 2;
  while (start <= Math.sqrt(item)) {
```

```
   if (item % start++ < 1) {

      return false;

   }

 }

 return item > 1;

}
document.writeln([4, 6, 11,

26].find(checkPrime));
</script>
```

The function will find 11 as the prime number.

forEach()

This method helps us to invoke a certain function once for every array element. It takes the syntax given below:

```
array.forEach(callback(current-value, index,
arr),thisArg)
```

The **callback** is the function for testing the condition. The **current-value** denotes the current element of the array. The *index* parameter is optional and it denotes the index of the current element. The **arr** parameter denotes the array to which we are to apply the function. The **thisArg** is an optional parameter. This is the value to be used as this during execution of the callback.

The method will return undefined.

For example:

```
<script>
var array1 = ['Java', 'C#', 'Python'];
array1.forEach(function(values) {
   document.writeln(values);
});
</script>
```

We have used the *forEach()* method to access and print the elements of the array. The code prints the following:

Java C# Python

We can also use the same function to create a **Fibonacci series**. For example:

```
<script>
var addition = 0;
var array1 = [2, 8, 14, 24];
array1.forEach(function fibfunction(item) {
    addition = addition + item;
   document.writeln(addition);
});
</script>
```

The code will return a Fibonacci sequence of the array elements. Note that the Fibonacci is a sequential cumulative addition of elements. Here is the output:

12 20 34 58

pop()

This method will remove the last element from an array and return the element. It has the effect of changing the length of the array. It has a simple syntax as shown below:

```
array.pop()
```
It returns the last element of the specified array. Consider the following example:

```
<script>
var array1=["Java","C#","Python"];
document.writeln("Initial array:
"+array1+"<br>");
document.writeln("Popped out item:
"+array1.pop()+"<br>");
document.writeln("Final array: "+ array1);
</script>
```

The code will return the following:

```
Initial array: Java.C#.Python
Popped out item: Python
Final array: Java.C#
```

We can use a *for* loop to pop all the array elements.

For example:

```
<script>
var array1=["Java","C#","Python"];
var len=array1.length;
for(var i= ;i<=len;i++)
   {
document.writeln("Popped out element:
"+array1.pop()+"<br>");
   }
</script>
```

The code will print the following:

```
Popped out element: Python
Popped out element: C#
Popped out element: Java
```

reverse()

This method has the impact of changing the way the array items are ordered, and it returns the items in a reverse sequence. The first element of the array will become the last while the last item will become the first element. It takes a simple syntax as shown below:

```
array.reverse()
```

It returns the original items of the array arranged in reverse order. For example:

```
<script>
var array1=["Java","C#","Python"];
var rv=array1.reverse();
document.writeln(rv);
</script>
```

The code will return the following output:

Python.C#.Java

The elements of the array have been returned while arranged in reverse order.

String

In JavaScript, a string is a sequence of characters. In JavaScript, we can create strings in two ways, using a string literal and using a string object.

A string literal is created by use of double quotes. To create a string using a string literal, use the syntax given below:

```
var string_name="string value";
```

For example:

```
<script>
var st ="A string literal";
document.write(st);
</script>
```

The code will print the following:

A string literal

To create a string using a string object, use the **new** keyword. The syntax should be as shown below:

```
var string_name=new String("a string literal");
```

We have used the **new** keyword to create an instance of a string. Consider the example given below:

```
<script>
var st = new String("Hello, this is a string");
document.write(st);
</script>
```

The code will return the following result:

Hello, this is a string

Let us discuss the various methods associated with JavaScript strings:

`charAt()`

This method helps in finding the character value located at a certain index. The indexes begin from 0 and go up to *n-1*; where *n* is the total number of characters in the string. The value of the index cannot be a negative value, equal to or greater than the length of the string. The method takes the following syntax:

```
String.charAt(index)
```

The index represents the position of the character. The method returns a character.

For example:

```
<script>
var st="JavaScript";
document.writeln(st.charAt(5));
</script>
```

We have used the method to detect the character at index **5** of the string. The code will return **c.** Note that the indexes begin at 0 and end at **n-1**.

We can also use the method and not pass an index to it. This is demonstrated below:

```
<script>
var st="JavaScript";
document.writeln(st.charAt());
</script>
```

The code will simply print the first character of the string, which is **J**. The following code demonstrates how we can print the last character of the string:

```
<script>
var st="JavaScript";
document.writeln(st.charAt(st.length-1));
</script>
```

The code will return *t* as it's the last character of the string.

concat()

This method helps in joining two or more strings together to form a single string. Note that the method doesn't change the original string in any way. The method takes the syntax given below:

```
string.concat(string1, string2,...,string-n)
```

Note that the parameters to the method are the strings to be joined.

Consider the example given below:

```
<script>
var a="Java";
var b="Script";
document.writeln(a.concat(b));
</script>
```

The code will return the following upon execution:

JavaScript

We created two strings *a* and *b* and combined them using the
concat() method. The following example demonstrates how we
can combine three strings together:

```
<script>
var a="Java";
var b="Script";
var c=" Language"
document.writeln(a.concat(b,c));
</script>
```

Note that we created some space when writing the string
Language. There is also another way of doing it as shown below:

```
<script>
var a="Java";
var b="Script";
```

```
var c=" Language"
document.writeln(a.concat(b+" "+c));
</script>
```

indexOf()

This method can be used to search and return the position of a certain character in a string. Always remember that string characters begin at index **0**. If the character is not found, the method will return a **-1**.

For example:

```
<script>
var st="JavaScript is a scripting language";
document.write(st.indexOf('a'));
</script>
```

The code returns **1**. This is because the first character **"a"** was found at index **1**. It is possible for us to provide the index at which our search should start.

This is demonstrated below:

```
<script>
var st="JavaScript is a scripting language";
document.write(st.indexOf('a', ));
</script>
```

The code will return **14**. This is because we have stated that the search should begin at index **8** rather than from index 0.

Other than a single character, we can print the position of the first character of a certain string.

For example:

```
<script>
var st="JavaScript is a scripting language";
document.write(st.indexOf("script"));
</script>
```

The code will return **16**. This is the position of character s in the *script*. Note that the search is case sensitive; hence the Script in JavaScript will be skipped. You can use Script rather than the script in the search and you will get a different result.

To avoid this confusion, we can provide the JavaScript with the index from which the search should start:

```
<script>
var st="JavaScript is a scripting language";
document.write(st.indexOf("script", 6));
</script>
```

The search will now begin from index 6 rather than from index **0**.

We can try to search for an element that doesn't exist and see what happens:

```
<script>
var st="JavaScript is a scripting language";
document.write(st.indexOf("Language", 6));
</script>
```

The script will return a **-1**. This is because we don't have a Language string. However, we have a language.

search()

This method is used for the purpose of searching for regular expressions in a string. If no match is found, the method will return a **-1**. The method normally goes with the syntax given below:

```
string.search(regexp)
```

The parameter ***regexp*** denotes the expression that is to be searched. The method normally returns the position of the character you were searching for.

Consider the example given below:

```
<script>
var st="JavaScript is a scripting language";
document.writeln(st.search("language"));
</script>
```

The code will return **26**. The string ***language*** begins at index **26**.

Note that the search method is case sensitive.

The following example demonstrates this:

```
<script>
var st="JavaScript is one of the scripting
languages. Scripting is always easy.";
document.writeln(st.search(/Scripting/));
</script>
```

The code will return **46**. This is because it is searching for an uppercase s. To ignore the case sensitive nature of the search, we can use the i flag as shown below:

```
<script>
var st="JavaScript is one of the scripting
languages. Scripting is always easy.";
document.writeln(st.search(/Scripting/i));
</script>
```

The code will now return **25** rather than **46**. This is because the search is no longer case sensitive.

Let us now search for a regular expression that is not present in the string and see what will happen:

```
<script>
```

```
var st="JavaScript is one of the scripting
languages. Scripting is always easy.";
document.writeln(st.search(/programming/));
</script>
```

The code will return a **-1** because the regular expression was not found.

match()

This method helps us to match a string against a regular expression. A global search modifier can be used with the **match()** method to get all matching elements, otherwise, the method will only return the first element that is found.

The **match()** method takes the following syntax:

```
string.match(regexp)
```

The **regexp** is the regular expression that you need to search. Consider the following example:

```
<script>
var st="JavaScript";
document.writeln(st.match("Java"));
</script>
```

The code will return *Java* as the output:

```
Java
```

We can demonstrate how to use the global search to perform the search:

```
<script>
var st="JavaScript";
document.writeln(st.match(/Java/g));
</script>
```

The code will return the following upon execution:

```
Java
```

The **match()** method is case sensitive. However, we can turn this off by using the ignore flag. This is demonstrated below:

```
<script>
var st="JavaScript";
document.writeln(st.match(/java/gi));
</script>
```

The code will return the following upon execution:

```
Java
```

This shows that the search is no longer case sensitive as it was before.

Chapter 9- JavaScript Events

Events are the actions which JavaScript can detect. A good example is an **onmouseover** event, which JavaScript detects once a mouse is moved over some object. The **onload** event is triggered once a web page is loaded. In JavaScript, events and functions are used together. A function is triggered once an event has occurred. Other examples of events include closing a window, pressing a key, resizing a window and others.

onclick Event

This is a common event in JavaScript. It occurs once a user has clicked the left button of the mouse. One can add a warning, validation etc. against the event. Example:

```
<html>
   <head>
      <script type="text/javascript">
           function helloFunc() {
              alert("Hello World!")
           }
      </script>

   </head>
```

```
    <body>
    <p>Click the button below</p>
  <form>
<input type="button" onclick="helloFunc()"
value="Click Here" />
    </form>
    </body>
</html>
```

In the example, a simple form has been created. It should be as follows:

Click the button below

Click Here

Click the "Click Here" button and the function ***helloFunc*** will be invoked. Once clicked, you will see a pop up as shown below:

Hello World!

OK

onsubmit Event

This even is called when one has submitted a form. Form validation can be added to the event. This will help you validate data before it can be sent to a webserver.

Example:

```html
<html>
   <head>
     <script type="text/javascript">
              function formValidation() {
                 // validation code should be
added here
                 return either true or false
              }
   </script>
   </head>
   <body>
   <form method="POST" onsubmit="return
formValidation()">
           <input type="submit" value="Submit" />
      </form>
      </body>
</html>
```

Once the **Submit** button is clicked, the *formValidation* method will be called.

onmouseout and onmouseover

These events help you add attractive features to both text and images. The **onmouseover** event is triggered once a mouse is moved over an object. The **onmouseout** event is triggered once the mouse is moved out of the element.

Example:

```html
<html>
    <head>
        <script type="text/javascript">
            function overObject() {
                document.write ("Your Mouse is Over");
            }

             function outOfObject() {
                document.write ("Your Mouse is Out");
            }
        </script>
    </head>
    <body>
```

```
    <p>Bring your mouse in the division and
observe:</p>
    <div onmouseover="overObject()"
onmouseout="outOfObject()">
    <h2>Division</h2>
    </div>
      </body>
</html>
```

The code gives the following when executed:

Bring your mouse in the division and observe:

Division

Just move your mouse as instructed and see what happens. It will change to the following:

The Mouse is OverThe Mouse is Out

We have defined two functions, that is, **overObject** and **outOfObject**. These two functions have then been called in the following line:

```
<div onmouseover="overObject()"
onmouseout="outOfObject()">
```

Once a mouse is moved over the division, the **overObject** method will be called. Once the mouse is moved out of the object, the **outOfObject** method will be called. The **onmouseover="overObject()"** instructs the JavaScript to call the **overObject** function once the mouse is moved over the division, while the **onmouseout="outOfObject()">** instructs the JavaScript interpreter to call the **outOfObject** function once the mouse is moved out of the division.

Here is another example that changes the color of the text after mouse hover:

```html
<html>
<body>
<h1 onmouseover="style.color='yellow'"
onmouseout="style.color='black'">
Move your cursor over here</h1>
</body>
</html>
```

When you move the mouse cursor of the text, the text will change its color to yellow. If you move away from the mouse cursor, the text will change color to black.

onload and onunload

These two events are invoked when a user has entered or left a page. We can use the **onload** event to check the type and version of the visitor's browser. It is from there that we can load the right web page depending on the version. Both are good functions for dealing with cookies:

```html
<html>
<body onload="inspectCookies()">
<p id="example"></p>
<script>
function inspectCookies() {
  var txt = "";
  if (navigator.cookieEnabled == true) {
    txt = "Your browser has cookies enabled.";
  } else {
    txt = "your browser has cookies disabled.";
  }
  document.getElementById("example").innerHTML = txt;
}
</script>
</body>
</html>
```

If you run the above code, the output that you get will depend on whether your browser has cookies enabled or not.

onchange Event

This method is mostly used during the validation of form fields. The following example demonstrates how to use this method:

```
<html>
<head>
<script>
function testFunc() {
  var a = document.getElementById("name");
  a.value = a.value.toUpperCase();
}
</script>
</head>
<body>
Name: <input type="text" id="name"
onchange="testFunc()">
<p>Leave the input field and see your name
change to uppercase</p>
</body>
</html>
```

After running the code, you will get the following simple form:

Name:

Leave the input field and see your name change to uppercase

Just type your name in lowercase and move the mouse cursor from the input field by clicking outside. You will notice that your name will be transformed into uppercase:

Name: JOHN

Leave the input field and see your name change to uppercase

The **upperCase()** method is invoked after the user has changed the content of the input field.

onload

When used, it displays an alert box after a page has been loaded. For example:

```
<html>
<head>
<script>
function displayMessage() {
  alert("A message by the onload event");
}
</script>
</head>
<body onload="displayMessage()">
</body>
</html>
```

Once the page has been loaded, you will get the following alert box:

A message by the onload event

OK

onfocus

This method makes an input field change its color after it gets focus.

Here is an example:

```
<html>
<head>
<script>
function myFunc(col) {
  col.style.background = "green";
}
</script>
</head>
<body>
Name: <input type="text" onfocus="myFunc(this)">
<p>Click inside the input field and see it
change color.</p>
```

```
</body>
</html>
```

The code will give you the following on execution:

Name: [   ]

Click inside the input field and see it change color.

You can then click inside the input field as instructed and see what happens. It will change color as follows:

Name: [▓▓▓▓▓▓▓▓▓▓▓▓▓▓▓▓▓]

Click inside the input field and see it change color.

The color of the input field will change into the green.

Chapter 10- JavaScript Validation

With JavaScript, one can validate a form before they can submit it. Initially, form validation was done on the side of the server. The user could fill a form then send it to a server. If the details were found to be wrong, the server had to send them back to the user for corrections. This process is too lengthy.

However, JavaScript has changed and improved how this is done. Validation of forms can be done on the client side before the form details can be submitted to the server. In form validation, we should ensure all the required fields are filled. Fields taking specific data formats such as emails, mobile phone numbers and other should be checked to ensure the format is adhered to. The validation of the form is normally done on submit.

Example:

```
<html>
<head>
</head>
<script type="text/javascript" >
 function formValidation(){
var name=document.detailsForm.username.value;
```

```
var
password=document.detailsForm.userpassword.value
;

if (name==null || name==""){
  alert("You MUST enter your name!");
  return false;
}else if(password.length<8){
  alert("You MUSt enter a password with 8
characters and above!");
  return false;
  }
}
</script>
<body>
<form name="detailsForm" method="post"
action="nm.jsp" onsubmit="return
formValidation()" >
Name: <input type="text" name="username"><br/>
Password: <input type="password"
name="userpassword"><br/>
<input type="submit" value="Login">
</form>
</body>
</html>
```

The code returns a simple form as shown below:

Name:
Password:
[Login]

Click the Login button without entering a value in any of the input fields; you will get the following alert box:

You MUST enter your name!

[OK]

This means that you must enter your name before proceeding. Now, enter your name but don't enter a password. You will get the following alert box:

You MUSt enter a password with 8 characters and above1

[OK]

This means that you must enter a password with **8** characters and above. You can now enter a short password and see whether the validation is working correctly. Enter a password with less than 8 characters then click the Login button. You will still get the above dialog.

We have created a form named ***detailsForm***. The form requires the user to enter his name and password. We have created the ***formValidation*** method to validate the values entered in the form. Username must be provided while the password should not have less than 8 characters. The property ***onsubmit=" return formValidation()"*** means that once the user clicks the **"Login"** button, the ***formValidation()*** method will be called so as to validate the details entered in the form. If they don't conform to the requirements, it will return false, so the user will have to re-enter the details.

Validating Retype Password

When a user is creating a password, they are normally asked to retype it to ensure they have mastered it well. This logic can be implemented in JavaScript as follows:

```
<script type="text/javascript" >
    function passwordMatch(){
    var
firstpassword=document.myform.userpassword1.valu
e;
```

```
    var
secondpassword=document.myform.userpassword2.val
ue;
   if(firstpassword==secondpassword){
     return true;
     }
     else{
     alert("The two passwords don't much!");
     return false;
     }
     }
     </script>
     <form name="myform" action="register.jsp"
onsubmit="return passwordMatch()">
     Password:<input type="password"
name="userpassword1" /><br/>
     Re-enter Password:<input type="password"
name="userpassword2"/><br/>
     <input type="submit">
     </form>
```

This returns the following simple form:

Password:
Re-enter Password:
Submit Query

Try to enter different passwords in the two fields then see what will happens after clicking the **"Submit Query"** button. You will get the following message:

The two passwords don't much!

OK

Number Validation

When requiring a user to enter a number such as age in a particular text field, you should validate the input to ensure they only enter a number.

This is demonstrated below:

```
<script type="text/javascript" >
 function formValidation(){

var number=document.form1.num.value;

if (isNaN(number)){


document.getElementById("mynum").innerHTML="Inpu
t must be a number!";

  return false;

}else{

  return true;
```

```
    }
}
</script>
<form name="form1" onsubmit="return
formValidation()" >
Number: <input type="text" name="num"><span
id="mynum"></span><br/>
<input type="submit" value="submit">
</form>
```

The *isNaN()* method is used in JavaScript to check whether a value is a number or not. We have used it in the above script. Run the code and you will get a form with an input field and a button as shown below:

Number:
submit

Enter a non-number value in the input field then click the Submit button. You will see the following message:

Number: jane   Input must be a number!
submit

The code returns the specified message if the input is not a number.

Email validation

JavaScript can be used for validation of email addresses. The following are the properties of a valid email address:

- It must the @ and. **(dot)** symbols
- There should be a character before @. as well as after.
- There must be not less than two characters after the **(dot).**

Example:

```
<script type="text/javascript" >
    function emailValidation()
{
var i=document.form1.emailAddress.value;
var atposition=i.indexOf("@");
var dotposition=i.lastIndexOf(".");
if (atposition<1 || dotposition<atposition+2 ||
dotposition+2>=i.length){
  alert("Please provide valid e-mail address \n
atpostion:"+atposition+"\n
dotposition:"+dotposition);
  return false;
  }
}
</script>
<body>
```

```html
<form name="form1"  method="post" action="#"
onsubmit="return emailValidation();">
Email: <input type="text"
name="emailAddress"><br/>
  <input type="submit" value="Submit Mail">
</form>
```

The code returns the following after execution:

Email:

Submit Mail

Try to type an invalid email address and click the Submit Mail button. See what happens. You should get the following alert box:

Please provide valid e-mail address
  atpostion:-1
  dotposition:-1

OK

validation with image

You may need to show different images based on whether the input is correct or wrong.

This can be implemented in JavaScript as follows:

```
<script type="text/javascript" >
  function formValidation(){
var name=document.form1.name.value;
var password=document.form1.password.value;
var status=false;
if(name.length<1){
document.getElementById("namespan").innerHTML=
" <img src='unchecked.gif'/> Please provide your
name";
status=false;
}else{
document.getElementById("namespan").innerHTML="
<img src='checked.gif'/>";
status=true;
}
if(password.length<8){
document.getElementById("passwordspan").innerHTM
L=
" <img src='unchecked.gif'/> Password should be
at least 8 char long";
status=false;
}else{
```

```
document.getElementById("passwordspan").innerHTM
L=" <img src='checked.gif'/>";
}
return status;
}
</script>


<form name="form1" action="#" onsubmit="return
formValidation()">
<table>
<tr><td>Enter Name:</td><td><input type="text"
name="name"/>
<span id="namespan"></span></td></tr>
<tr><td>Enter Password:</td><td><input
type="password" name="password"/>
<span id="passwordspan"></span></td></tr>
<tr><td colspan="2"><input type="submit"
value="Login"/></td></tr>
</table>
</form>
```

The script returns the following simple form upon execution:

Enter Name:

Enter Password:

Login

Click the Login button without entering the username or the password. You will see the images alongside the relevant messages.

Enter Name: [   ] 🖼 Please provide your name

Enter Password: [   ] 🖼 Password should be at least 8 char long

[Login]

Chapter 11- The Document Object Model

The document object refers to your whole HTML page. After you load an object into the web browser, it immediately becomes a document object, which is the root element representing the html document. It comes with both properties and methods. The document object helps us add content to the web pages.

It is an object of the window, which means that having:

`window.document`

Is the same as having?

`document`

DOM Methods

DOM methods are the actions that you can perform on the html elements. The **DOM** properties are the values of the **HTML** elements which one can set or change. The following are the document object methods:

1. **write("string")**- it writes a string to a document.
2. **writeln("string")**- it writes a string to a document with a new line character.
3. **getElementById()**- gives the element with the specified id.

4. **getElementsByName()**-gives all the elements with the specified name.

5. **getElementsByTagName()**-gives all the elements with the specified tag name.

6. **getElementsByClassName()**-gives all the elements with the specified class name.

Accessing Field Values

The DOM is a good way of getting the values of an input field. Many are the times you will need to get input from a user. This can be done using the following property:

```
document.formname.name.value
```
Where:

- **document**- is the html document representing our root element.
- **form_name**- is the name of the form with the fields.
- **field_name**- is the name of the input text.
- **value**- is a property which returns the value of input text.

Consider the following example:

```
<html>
<body>
<script type="text/javascript">
```

```
    function readValue(){
    var
name=document.memberform.memberName.value;
    alert("Hi: "+name);
    }
</script>

    <form name="memberform">
    Enter Name:<input type="text"
name="memberName"/>
    <input type="button" onclick="readValue()"
value="Click Here"/>
    </form>
</body>
</html>
```

When you run the code, it will give you the following simple form:

Enter Name: _____   [Click Here]

Just enter your name in the input field and click the Click Here button. See what happens.

You will get an alert box with your name and some text appended to it:

Hi: John

OK

We simply created a simple form with an input text field. The method ***readValue()*** helps us get the value that we enter into the field. Consider the following line:

```
var name=document.memberform.memberName.value;
```

The ***memberName*** is the name given to the text field in the form, and these must match, otherwise, you will not the right results.

getElementById()

Other than the name, we can also get the element by its id. This can be done using the ***document.getElementById()*** method. However, the input text field should be given an id.

 For example:

```
<html>
<body>
```

```
<script type="text/javascript">
    function computeSquare(){
    var
x=document.getElementById("integer").value;
    alert(x * x);
    }
</script>
<form>
    Enter an Integer:<input type="text"
id="integer" name="myNumber"/><br/>
    <input type="button" value="Compute Square"
onclick="computeSquare()"/>
</form>
</body>
</html>
```

The code should give you the following simple form upon execution:

Enter an Integer:

Compute Square

Enter a number in the input field and click the Compute Square button.

This should return the square of the number in a popup box as shown below:

81

> OK

In the example, we have defined the ***computeSquare()*** method which helps us get the square of a number entered in the input text field. Consider the following line:

```
var x=document.getElementById("integer").value;
```

In the line, we have used the ***getElementById()*** method which takes the id of the input text field as the argument. The method helps us get the value typed in the input text field using its id.

getElementsByName()

The ***document.getElementsByName()*** method can help us get an element by its name. The method has the syntax given below:

```
document.getElementsByName("name")
```

The name is needed.

Example:

```
<html>
<body>
<script type="text/javascript">
    function getNumber()
    {
    var
options=document.getElementsByName("option");
    alert("Total Options:"+options.length);
    }
    </script>
    <form>
    Yes:<input type="radio" name="option"
value="yes">
    No:<input type="radio" name="option"
value="no">
     <input type="button" onclick="getNumber()"
value="Available Options">
</form>
</body>
</html>
```

Upon execution, the code returns the following:

Yes: ◉ No: ◌   ⬜ Available Options

Click the Available Options button and see what happens. A popup window will be shown as follows:

Total Options:2

```
OK
```

We have created two radio buttons with options **Yes** and **No**. Note that these two input types have been given the same name, that is, *option*.

Consider the following line:

```
var
options=document.getElementsByName("option");
```

The line helps us count the number of elements with the name *option*. This should be **2** as shown in the output.

getElementsByTagName()

The ***document.getElementsByTagName()*** property returns the elements with the tag name which is specified. It takes the syntax given below:

```
document.getElementsByTagName("name")
```

For example:

```
<html>
<body>
<script type="text/javascript">
function allparagraphs(){
var pgs=document.getElementsByTagName("p");
alert("Total paragraphs are: "+pgs.length);
}
</script>
    <p>This is a paragraph</p>
    <p>This is a paragraph</p>
    <p>This is a paragraph</p>
    <p>This is a paragraph</p>
<button onclick="allparagraphs()">Total
Paragraphs</button>
</body>
</html>
```

The code returns the following upon execution:

This is a paragraph

This is a paragraph

This is a paragraph

This is a paragraph

Total Paragraphs

Click the Total Paragraphs button and see what happens.

You will see the following popup:

Total paragraphs are: 4

OK

This means that the code was able to count the number of paragraphs that we have.

The main logic lies in the following line:

```
var pgs=document.getElementsByTagName("p");
```

We have passed the tag **"p"** as the argument to our method, and the tag represents a paragraph. There are three elements with the tag **"p"**, so the output should be **4** paragraphs.

 Here is another example:

```
< html>

<body>

<script type="text/javascript">
function countheader2(){
```

```
var h2count=document.getElementsByTagName("h2");
alert("Total count for h2 tags:
"+h2count.length);
}
function countheader3(){
var h3count=document.getElementsByTagName("h3");
alert("Total count for h3 tags:
"+h3count.length);
}
</script>
<h2>A h2 tag</h2>
<h2>A h2 tag</h2>
<h2>A h2 tag</h2>
<h2>A h2 tag</h2>
<h3>A h3 tag</h3>
<h3>A h3 tag</h3>
<h3>A h3 tag</h3>
<h3>A h3 tag</h3>
<h3>A h3 tag</h3>
<button onclick="countheader2()">Total
h2</button>
<button onclick="countheader3()">Total
h3</button>
</body>
</html>
```

The code returns the following output upon execution:

A h2 tag

A h2 tag

A h2 tag

A h2 tag

A h3 tag

A h3 tag

A h3 tag

A h3 tag

A h3 tag

| Total h2 | Total h3 |

We have a total of **4 h2** tags and a total of **5 h3** tags. Click the Total **h2** button and see what happens.

You should get the following popup box:

Total count for h2 tags: 4

OK

Click the Total **h3** button and see what happens.

You should get the following popup box:

Total count for h3 tags: 5

OK

innerHTML

This property can be used for addition of a dynamic content to an html page. It is used on html pages when there is a need to generate a dynamic content like comment form, registration form, etc.

 Consider the following example:

```
<html>
<body>
<script type="text/javascript" >
function displayform() {
var data="Username:<br><input type='text'
name='name'><br>Comment:<br><textarea rows='6'
cols='45'></textarea><br><input type='submit'
value='Contact us'>";
document.getElementById('area').innerHTML=data;
 }
```

```
</script>
<form name="form1">
<input type="button" value="Contact us"
onclick="displayform()">
<div id="area"></div>
</form>
</body>
</html>
```

The code returns the following button upon execution:

Contact us

Click the button and see what happens. You will get the following:

What we have done is that we are creating a contact us form after the user has clicked a button. Note that the html form has been generated within a div that we have created and given it the name *area*. To identify the position, we have called the **document.getElementById()** method.

innerText

We can use this property to add a dynamic property into an HTML page. Note that when this property is used, your text is interpreted as a normal text rather than as html content. A good application of this is when you need to write the strength of a password based on its length, write a validation message etc.

For example:

```
<html>
<body>
<script type="text/javascript" >
function validatePass() {
var message;
if(document.form1.userPass.value.length>5){
message="good";
}
else{
message="poor";
}
document.getElementById('area').innerText=messag
e;
 }
</script>
<form name="form1">
```

```
<input type="password" value="" name="userPass"
onkeyup="validatePass()">
Strength:<span id="area"> Pasword strength
</span>
</form>
</body>
</html>
```

The code returns the following upon execution:

Strength: Pasword strength

Just begin to type the password and see what happens to the text on the right of the input field as you type. If you type less than 5 characters for the password, the message will change to poor as shown below:

Strength:poor

Continue to type the password until you have more than 5 characters. You will see the message change to good as shown below:

Strength:good

That is how powerful this property is.

Animations

With JavaScript, we can animate elements. We can use JavaScript to move elements such as **<img />**, **<div>** etc. on a page depending on an equation. The following are the common methods used for animations in JavaScript:

1. **setTimeout(method, time)**- this method will call the *method* after some*time* in milliseconds.
2. **setInterval (method, time)**- the method will call the *method* after *time* milliseconds.

With JavaScript, one can set some attributes of the **DOM** object such its position on the screen. The position of the object can be set using *top* and *left* attributes.

This is demonstrated below:

```
// Set the distance from the left edge of the
screen.
object.style.left = distance measures in points
or pixels;
```
or

```
// Set the distance from the top edge of screen.
object.style.top = distance measures in points
or pixels;
```

Manual Animation

In the following example, we will be animating the image towards the right:

```html
<html>
<body>
<script type="text/javascript">
            var image = null;
                function init(){
            image =
document.getElementById('myImage');
            image.style.position= 'relative';
            image.style.left = '0px';
            }
                function moveImage(){
             image.style.left =
parseInt(image.style.left) + 10 + 'px';
            }
            window.onload =init;
     </script>
     </head>
   <body>
   <form>
   <img id="myImage" src="house.jpg" />
```

```
    <p>Click the button to move the image</p>
<input type="button" value="Move Image"
onclick="moveImage();" />
    </form>
</body>
</html>
```

You should use the correct name of your image in the following line:

```
<img id="myImage" src="house.jpg" />
```

In my case, I have a .jpg image named *house*. When I run the code, it returns the following:

Click the button to move the image

Move Image

Click the **"Move Image"** button. The image should move to the right with each click. This is shown below:

Click the button to move the image

Move Image

Consider the following line in the script:

```
image = document.getElementById('myImage');
```

We are getting the image using its **ID**, then it is assigned to the *image* variable. The *init()* method helps us set the initial position of the image on the window. The method will be called when the window is being loaded. The *moveImage()* function will move the image towards the right by **10 pixels** after every click. To move the image towards the left, the value should be set as negative. The animation, in this case, is manual as we have to click a button.

Automated Animation

To automate the process of animating an element, we can use the *setTimeout()* function provided by JavaScript.

Example:

```html
<script type="text/javascript">
        var image = null;
        var animate ;
        function init(){
            image =
document.getElementById('myImage');
            image.style.position= 'relative';
            image.style.left = '0px';
        }
        function animateImage(){
          image.style.left =
parseInt(image.style.left) + 10 + 'px';
            animate =
setTimeout(animateImage,20);
        }
        function stopAnimation(){
```

```
            clearTimeout(animate);

            image.style.left = '0px';

        }
        window.onload =init;
    </script>
  </head>
  <body>
    <form>
            <img id="myImage" src="house.jpg " />
            <p>Click the Animate button to launch
animation</p>
            <input type="button" value="Animate"
onclick="animateImage();" />
            <input type="button" value="Stop"
onclick="stopAnimation();" />
        </form>
```

The code returns the following upon execution:

Click the Animate button to launch animation

Animate   Stop

Click the **"Animate"** button. The animation should start. When you click the Stop button, the animation will stop.

The *animateImage()* method is calling the *setTimeout* method which sets the position of the image after every 20 milliseconds. This will result in the animation of the image. The *stopAnimation()* method helps in clearing the timer which is set by the *setTimeout()* method. The object, which is the image, is set back to its initial position.

Rollover

We can use a mouse image to rollover an image in JavaScript. Once you move the mouse over the image, it will change to another image.

Example:

```html
<html>
<body>
<script type="text/javascript">
            if(document.images){
                var img1 = new Image();
                img1.src = "ps.jpg";
                var img2 = new Image();
                img2.src = "house.jpg";
            }
        </script>
    </head>
    <body>
        <p>Move mouse over to rollover</p>
<a href="#"
onMouseOver="document.img.src=img2.src;"
onMouseOut="document.img.src=img1.src;">
        <img name="img" src="nicsam.jpg" />
        </a>
</body>
</html>
```

We have used the *if* statement to check whether the image exists or not. We have the used the ***Image()*** constructor so as to preload some new object named ***img1***. The same has also been done to preload the second image, ***img2***. The *src* is given the name of the image stored externally. The # helps to disable the link so that a URL is not opened once it is clicked. The method *onMouseOver* is called once the mouse cursor is moved over the image. The *onMouseOut* method will be called once the mouse cursor is moved out of the image.

Chapter 12- Browser Object Model

The **BOM (Browser Object Model)** is used for interaction with the browser. The default browser object is a *window*, meaning that you can call all window functions directly or by specifying the window. We had discussed this, so we will not revisit it. Other than the window object, there are various other BOM objects. Let us discuss them:

History Object

This object keeps an array of all URLs that the user has visited. You can use this object to load web pages, previous, forward and any certain web page. This object can be accessed as shown below:

```
window.history
```

It can also be accessed as follows:

`history`

This object has only one property, which is the **_length_** and it returns the length of history URLs. The history object has **3** methods which include the following:

- **forward()**- it will load the next page
- **back()**- it will   load the previous page
- **go()**- it will load a given page number.

The history object can be used in the following various ways:

1. **history.back();**//for previous page
2. **history.forward();**//for next page
3. **history.go(2);**//for next 2nd page
4. **history.go(-2);**//for previous 2nd page

Navigator Object

This object is used for detecting browsers. It can help get information about the browser in terms of **appName**, **userAgent**, **appCodeName** etc.

The navigator object is a property of the window, and we can access it as follows:

```
window.navigator
```

It can also be accessed as follows:

```
navigator
```

The object comes with various properties including the following:

- **appName**- it returns the name
- **appCodeName**- it returns code name
- **appVersion**- it returns the version
- **cookieEnabled**- it returns true if browser cookies are enabled and false otherwise

- **language**- it returns the language. Supported in Firefox and Netscape only.
- **userAgent**- it returns user agent
- **userLanguage**- it returns the users' language. It's supported only in IE.
- **systemLanguage**- it returns system language. Supported only in IE.
- **Plugins**- it returns the plugins. Supported in Firefox and Netscape only.
- **mimeTypes[]**- it returns an array of mime type. Supported in Firefox and Netscape only.
- **online**- it returns true if the browser is online and false otherwise.
- **platform**- it returns the platform such as Win32.

The navigator object has the following methods:

- **javaEnabled()**- it checks whether java has been enabled.
- **taintEnabled()**- it checks whether taint has been enabled. Deprecated from JavaScript 1.2.

Consider the navigator object example given below:

```
<script>
document.writeln("<br/>navigator.appName:
"+navigator.appName);
```

```
document.writeln("<br/>navigator.appCodeName:
"+navigator.appCodeName);
document.writeln("<br/>navigator.appVersion:
"+navigator.appVersion);
document.writeln("<br/>navigator.language:
"+navigator.language);
document.writeln("<br/>navigator.cookieEnabled:
"+navigator.cookieEnabled);
document.writeln("<br/>navigator.userAgent:
"+navigator.userAgent);
document.writeln("<br/>navigator.onLine:
"+navigator.onLine);
document.writeln("<br/>navigator.platform:
"+navigator.platform);
</script>
```

The code returns the following details:

```
navigator.appName: Netscape
navigator.appCodeName: Mozilla
navigator.appVersion: 5.0 (Windows)
navigator.language: en-US
navigator.cookieEnabled: true
navigator.userAgent: Mozilla/5.0 (Windows NT 6.1; WOW64; rv:52.0) Gecko/20100101 Firefox/52.0
navigator.onLine: true
navigator.platform: Win32
```

Note that the output will depend on the kind of operating system, the browser you are using and other details.

Screen Object

This JavaScript object keeps information about the screen of the browser. You can use it to display details of the screen such as the **height**, **width**, **pixelDepth**, **colorDepth** etc. It is a property of the window object, hence we access as follows:

```
window.screen
```

We can also access it as follows:

```
screen
```

The object has many properties including the following:

- **width**- it returns the width of the browser screen
- **height**- it returns the height of browser screen
- **availWidth**- it prints the available width
- **availHeight**- it prints available height
- **colorDepth**- it returns color depth
- **pixelDepth**- it returns pixel depth.

The following example shows how this object can be used:

```
<script>
document.writeln("<br/>screen.height: "+screen.height);
document.writeln("<br/>screen.width: "+screen.width);
```

```
document.writeln("<br/>screen.availHeight:
"+screen.availHeight);
document.writeln("<br/>screen.availWidth:
"+screen.availWidth);
document.writeln("<br/>screen.pixelDepth:
"+screen.pixelDepth);
document.writeln("<br/>screen.colorDepth:
"+screen.colorDepth);
</script>
```

The code returns the following after execution:

screen.height: 768
screen.width: 1366
screen.availHeight: 728
screen.availWidth: 1366
screen.pixelDepth: 24
screen.colorDepth: 24

Page Printing

Sometimes, you may need to send the contents of a particular web page to a printer for printing. This can be done by adding a button which users will have to click in order to print. This can be implemented using the **print** method of **window** object. When the **window.print()** function is called, the current page will be printed. The function can be called using **onClick()** event.

Example:

```
<html>
      <body>
      <form>
          <input type="button" value="Print Page"
onclick="window.print()" />
    </body>
</html>
```

Execute the script and you will see the following button:

Print Page

 Click the **"Print Page"** button. The page will be send to the printer for printing. You will be asked to specify the various printing options.

Chapter 13- JavaScript Cookies

Cookies refer to the data kept in text files on a computer. During browsing, a web page is sent to the user's browser, and the web server forgets this. Cookies help in remembering information regarding users. Once a user has visited a webpage, a cookie can help to store his name. The user will be remembered the next time he visits the page. They are saved using name-value pairs as shown below:

```
username = John Joel
```

Once a user's browser requests for a page from the server, the page's cookies are added to the request. The server will then all the information it needs to remember users.

Creating Cookies

The JavaScript ***document.cookie*** can be used for creation, deletion, and reading of a cookie.

Example:

```
document.cookie = "username=John joel";
```

An expiry date for the cookie can also be added in **UTC**. After closing a browser, the cookie becomes deleted.

Example:

```
document.cookie = "username=John Joel;
expires=Fri, 22 Feb 2019 12:00:00 UTC";
```

That is how you can specify the expiry date of a cookie. The path for a cookie can also be specified.

Example:

```
document.cookie = "username=John Joel;
expires=Fri, 22 Feb 2019 12:00:00 UTC; path=/";
```

The following script demonstrates this:

```
<html>
<body>
     <script type = "text/javascript">
          function CreateCookie()
          {
               if( document.form1.field.value ==
"" ){
                    alert("Type a value");
                    return;
               }
value= escape(document.form1.field.value) + ";";
document.cookie="name=" + value;
document.write ("Creating Cookies: " + "name=" +
value );
          }
```

```
        </script>

    </head>

    <body>

        <form name="form1" action="">
            Name: <input type="text" name="field"/>
            <input type="button" value="Create
Cookie" onclick="CreateCookie();"/>
        </form>

</body>
</html>
```

The code will return the following form after execution:

Enter name: _____   [Create Cookie]

Type a name in the field then click the **"Create Cookie"** button. You should see the following:

Creating Cookies: name=John%20Joel;

The cookie will be created. You will then have a cookie with the name you typed in your computer. If you need to create many cookies at once, separate them using commas.

Reading Cookies

Cookies can be rea using **document cookie** object. The cookie name is passed to the object. The string may be used anytime you are in need of accessing the cookie. The string **document. cookie** stores cookies in the form **name=value** pairs then separated using semicolons. The **name** represents the name of the cookie, while the **value** denotes the string value.

With the **split()** function, one is able to break the string to get keys and values.

Example:

```
<script type="text/javascript">
        function ReadCookies()
        {
            var cookies = document.cookie;
            document.write ("Cookies include:
" + cookies );


            myArray = cookies.split(';');


            for(var x=0; x<myArray.length;
x++){
                name =
myArray[x].split('=')[0];
```

```
                    value =
myArray[x].split('=')[1];
                    document.write ("The Key is :
" + name +" and Value is : " + value);
                }
            }
        </script>
    </head>
    <body>

        <form name="form1" action="">
            <p> Click the button to see result:</p>
            <input type="button" value="Read
Cookie" onclick="ReadCookies()"/>
</form>
```

Execute the script and you will see the following interface:

Click the button to see result:

Read Cookie

Click the **"Read Cookie"** button. All cookies will be shown in the output.

Cookies include: name=John%20Joel; _ga=GA1.1.1074246533.1546774554; _utma=1.1074246533.1546774554.1546774554.1546774554.1; _utmz=1.1546774554.1.1.utmcsr=(direct)|utmccn=(direct)|utmcmd=(none); _cb_ls=1; _cb=mOO3YC8AjFYBdCBJe; _chartbeat2=.1546774595422.1546774595422.1.sx2NC0T2yFBVZp6ECKTrvT88_ka The Key is : name and Value is : John%20Joel The Key is :_ga and Value is : GA1.1.1074246533.1546774554 The Key is :_utma and Value is : 1.1074246533.1546774554.1546774554.1546774554.1 The Key is : _utmz and Value is : 1.1546774554.1.1.utmcsr The Key is :_cb_ls and Value is : 1 The Key is :_cb and Value is : mOO3YC8AjFYBdCBJe The Key is :_chartbeat2 and Value is : .1546774595422.1546774595422.1.sx2NC0T2yFBVZp6ECKTrvT88_ka

The **length** in this case gives us the array length.

Deleting Cookies

Sometimes, you may not need a cookie to be read. This calls for you to delete it. The deletion of an array involves assigning to it an expiry date which is past the current date.

Example:

```
<script type="text/javascript">
        function CreateCookie()
        {
            var time = new Date();
            time.setMonth( time.getMonth() -
1 );
            value =
escape(document.form1.field.value) + ";"

            document.cookie="name=" + value;
            document.cookie = "expires=" +
time.toUTCString() + ";"
            document.write("Set the Cookies :
" + "name=" + value );
        }
    </script>
 </head>
```

```
<body>
    <form name="form1" action="">
        Enter name: <input type="text"
name="field"/>
        <input type="button" value="Create
Cookie" onclick="CreateCookie()"/>
    </form>
```

In the example, we have deleted the cookie by setting its expiry date to last one month. This logic has been achieved in the following line of the code:

```
time.setMonth( time.getMonth() - 1 );
```

Chapter 14- Object Oriented Programming

JavaScript supports the concepts of object oriented programming. Let us discuss them:

Classes

JavaScript classes are a special type of JavaScript functions. Classes can be defined in the same way as functions and function expressions.

A JavaScript class has many members, include methods or constructors. A JavaScript class is executed in the strict mode. So any code with silent mistake or error will throw an error.

A class syntax is made up of two components:

- **Class declarations**
- **Class expressions**

Class Declarations

To declare a class, we use a class declaration. This is done using the *class* keyword followed by the class name. the JavaScript naming conventions require that the name of a class should begin with an uppercase letter.

Here is an example of a class declaration in JavaScript:

```
<script>
//Declare a class
class Student
  {
//Initialize an object
    constructor(admission, name)
    {
      this.admission=admission;
      this.name=name;
    }
//Declare a method
    detail()
    {
  document.writeln(this.admission+"
"+this.name+"<br>")
    }
  }
//pass an object to the variable
var student1=new Student(3380,"John Joel");
var student2=new Student(102,"Mercy George");
student1.detail(); //call a method
student2.detail();
</script>
```

The code returns the following upon execution:

```
3380 John Joel
102 Mercy George
```

We have created a class named **Student**. We have then initialized a constructor with two arguments, **admission** and **name**. We have then created a method named **detail()** which should return the details of the student, including the admission and the name. Consider the following two lines extracted from the code:

```
var student1=new Student(3380,"John Joel");
var student2=new Student(102,"Mercy George");
```

What we are doing is known as **instantiation**. We are simply creating an instance/object of type **Student**. This means that **student1** is an instance of Student, hence he can access all the properties defined within the Student class. This also applies to **student2**. The details of each student have been passed as arguments. We have lastly invoked the **detail()** method to return the details of each student.

Unlike the declaration of a function, the declaration of a class is not part of the JavaScript hoisting. This means that you are expected to declare a class before you can invoke it.

This is demonstrated in the following example:

```
<script>
//Here, we invoke the class before we declare
it.
var student1=new Student(3380,"John Joel");
var student2=new Student(102,"Mercy George");
student1.detail(); //call a method
student2.detail();

//Declare the class
class Student
  {
//Initialize an object
    constructor(admission, name)
    {
      this.admission=admission;
      this.name=name;
    }
//Declare a method
    detail()
    {
  document.writeln(this.admission+"
"+this.name+"<br>")
    }
  }
```

```
</script>
```

The above code cannot work as we have tried to access a class before declaring it.

A class can only be declared once. If you try to declare it more than once, it will return an error.

Here is an example:

```
<html>
<body>
<script>
//Declare a class

class Student
  {
//Initialize an object
    constructor(admission, name)
    {
      this.admission=admission;
      this.name=name;
    }
//Declare a method
    detail()
    {
  document.writeln(this.admission+"
"+this.name+"<br>")
    }
```

```
   }
//pass an object to the variable
var student1=new Student(3380,"John Joel");
var student2=new Student(102,"Mercy George");
student1.detail();  //call a method
student2.detail();
//Re-declaring class
class Student
   {
   }
</script>
</body>
</html>
```

The above code will also not run as we have declared the class **_Student_** twice.

Class expressions

A class can also be defined using a class expression. In such a case, the class name is not mandatory. This means that you can have a named or unnamed class expression. The class expression will allow you to fetch the name of the class. However, a class declaration doesn't allow this.

Here is an example of unnamed class expression:

```
<script>
var stud = class {
   constructor(admission, name) {
      this.admission = admission;
      this.name = name;

   }
};
document.writeln(stud.name);
</script>
```

Upon execution, the code will return the following:

stud

The class has been assigned to a variable rather than being given a name.

With a class expression, it is possible for us to re-declare a class.

```
<script>
//Declare a class
var stud=class
   {
//Initialize an object
      constructor(admission, name)
      {
         this.admission=admission;
         this.name=name;
```

```
      }
//Declare a method
detail()
      {
  document.writeln(this.admission+"
"+this.name+"<br>")
      }
   }
//pass an object to the variable
var student1=new stud(3380,"John Joel");
var student2=new stud(102,"Mercy George");
student1.detail(); //calling the method
student2.detail();


//Re-declare the class
var stud=class
   {
//Initialize an object
      constructor(admission, name)
      {
        this.admission=admission;
        this.name=name;
      }
//Declare a method
detail()
```

```
    {
  document.writeln(this.admission+"
"+this.name+"<br>")
    }
  }
//pass an object to the variable
var student1=new stud(3380,"John Joel");
var student2=new stud(102,"Mercy George");
student1.detail(); //calling the method
student2.detail();
</script>
```

The code will return successfully to return the following result:

```
3380 John Joel
102 Mercy George
3380 John Joel
102 Mercy George
```

A class expression can be named. In such a case, the scope of the class name depends on the body of the class. To retrieve the class name, we use the property **class.name**. Consider the following example:

```
<script>
var stud = class Student {
  constructor(admission, name) {
    this.admission = admission;
```

```
      this.name = name;

  }
};
document.writeln(stud.name);
```

```
</script>
```
The code runs successfully to return the following:

Student

Let us now try to write the code as follows:

```
<script>
var stud = class Student {
  constructor(admission, name) {
    this.admission = admission;
    this.name = name;

  }
};
document.writeln(Student.name);
</script>
```
The code will generate an error.

Objects

An object in JavaScript is an entity with both state and behavior, that is, properties and methods. An example of an object is a chair, a mouse, a keyboard, pen, etc.

JavaScript works based on objects. It treats everything as an object. It is template based rather than being class based. Classes are not created to get objects, but we can directly create objects.

JavaScript provides us with three ways through which we can create objects. These include the following:

1. Using object literal
2. Creating an instance of the Object directly (via the new keyword)
3. Using an object constructor (via the new keyword)

Using Object Literal

To create an object using an object literal, we use the syntax given below:

```
object={property1:value1,
property2:value2.....propertyN:valueN}
```

We use a colon (:) to separate the property from the value.

The following example demonstrates how this method can be used to create an object:

```
<script>
student={admission:3380, name:"John Joel",
age:28}
document.write(student.admission+"
"+student.name+" "+student.age);
</script>
```

The code returns the following result:

3380 John Joel 28

The output clearly shows that the JavaScript interpreter is able to know what the syntax means, in that the property comes first followed by the value. That is why it was able to get the values of the properties we need to access.

By creating an Object Instance

This is done using the following syntax:

```
var object_name=new Object();
```

Note that we have used the **new** keyword to create the object.

The following example demonstrates how we can create an object directly:

```
<script>
var stud=new Object();
stud.admission=3380;
stud.name="John Joel";
stud.age=28;
document.write(stud.admission+" "+stud.name+"
"+stud.age);
</script>
```

The code will print the following result:

3380 John Joel 28

Using Object Constructor

This involves creating a function with arguments. Every argument value can be assigned to the current object via **this** keyword which denotes the current object.

Consider the following example:

```
<script>
function stud(admission, name, age){
this.admission=admission;
this.name=name;
```

```
this.age=age;
}
s=new stud(3380,"John Joel",28);

document.write(s.admission+" "+s.name+"
"+s.age);
</script>
```

The code returns the following upon execution:

3380 John Joel 28

JavaScript allows us to define a method in an object. But before we can define the method, we should first define a property with the same name as the method.

The following example shows how we can define a method in an object:

```
<script>
function stud(admission, name, age){
this.admission=admission;
this.name=name;
this.age=age;
this.updateAge=updateAge;
function updateAge(newAge){
this.age=newAge;
}
```

```
}
s=new stud(3380,"John Joel",28);
document.write(s.admission+" "+s.name+" "+s.age
+ "<br>");
s.updateAge(29);
document.write(s.admission+" "+s.name+"
"+s.age);
</script>
```

The code will return the following result after execution:

```
3380 John Joel 28
3380 John Joel 29
```

We have defined the **updateAge()** method that helps us change the age of the student. In the example, the age of the student has been updated from **28** to **29**.

Prototype

JavaScript language works based on prototypes, allowing the objects to acquire features and properties from each other. Here, every object has a prototype object.

After the creation of a function in JavaScript, the prototype property gets added to that function automatically. The property is a prototype object holding the constructor property.

Here is the syntax for the creation of a prototype object in JavaScript:

```
ClassName.prototype.methodName
```

After creating an object, the functions that correspond to it are loaded into the memory. This means that a new copy of a function for every object. Thus, all functions are loaded into the memory at once.

Prototype Chaining

Each JavaScript object has a prototype object that acquires methods and properties from it. A prototype of an object may have a prototype object that can acquire methods and properties, and this continues. We can see this as **prototype chaining**.

The following example demonstrates how we can add a new method to a constructor function:

```
<script>
function Student(firstName,lastName)
{
   this.firstName=firstName;
   this.lastName=lastName;
}
Student.prototype.fullName=function()
   {
```

```
      return this.firstName+" "+this.lastName;
  }
var student1=new Student("John","Joel");
var student2=new Student("Mercy", "George");
document.writeln(student1.fullName()+"<br>");
document.writeln(student2.fullName());
</script>
```

The code returns the following result:

John Joel
Mercy George

The ***fullName()*** function combines the firstName and the lastName to return the full name of the student.

Let us create another example that demonstrates how to add a new property to a constructor function:

```
<script>
function Student(firstName,lastName)
{
   this.firstName=firstName;
   this.lastName=lastName;
}
Student.prototype.school="ABC"
var student1=new Student("John","Joel");
```

```
var student2=new Student("Mercy", "George");
document.writeln(student1.firstName+"
"+student1.lastName+" "+student1.school+"<br>");
document.writeln(student2.firstName+"
"+student2.lastName+" "+student2.school+"<br>");
</script>
```

The code should return the following result:

John Joel ABC
Mercy George ABC

We have created a prototype for *school* and all students are inheriting it. That is why they belong to **ABC school**.

Constructor Method

A constructor method is a special method in JavaScript used for initialization and creation of objects. It is called after the allocation of memory to an object.

The constructor method is declared using the *constructor* keyword. A class can only have one constructor method. The parent class constructor can be used via the ***super*** keyword.

The following example shows how to declare a constructor method:

```
<script>
class Student {
```

```
  constructor() {

    this.admission=3380;

    this.name = "John Joel";

  }

}

var stud = new Student();

document.writeln(stud.admission+" "+stud.name);

</script>
```

The code will return the following result after execution:

3380 John Joel

Note that the constructor has a body denoted by curly braces **{}**. It is within the body of the constructor that we have created and initialized the various properties.

As stated above, we can use the ***super*** keyword to call the constructor of the parent class.

Static Method

JavaScript provides us with static methods which only belong to the class but not to the class instances. This means that we don't need an instance to invoke a static method. We call these methods directly on the class.

A static method is declared using the *static* keyword. The method can take any name. A JavaScript class is allowed to have more than one static method. In case more than one static method is declared using one name, then the last method will be invoked after a call. A static method can be called within another static method using ***this*** keyword. A static method can be used for the creation of utility functions.

 Here is an example of a static method:

```
<script>
class StaticTest
{
  static show()
  {
    return "Static method has been invoked"
  }
}
document.writeln(StaticTest.show());
</script>
```

The code will print the following after execution:

 Static method has been invoked

The **show()** method has been declared using the **static** keyword, which makes it a static method. Let us see how one can invoke more than one static method:

```
<script>
class StaticTest
{
 static show1()
  {
    return "Static method has been invoked"
  }
 static show2()
  {
    return "Static method invoked again"
  }
}
document.writeln(StaticTest.show1()+"<br>");
document.writeln(StaticTest.show2());
</script>
```

The code will return the following once executed:

Static method has been invoked
Static method invoked again

We have created two static methods, **show1()** and **show()2**. We have then invoked them to get the result shown above.

We can create more than one static method with the same name
and invoke them. This is demonstrated below:

```
class StaticTest
{
  static show()
  {
    return "Static method has been invoked"
  }
  static show()
  {
    return "Static method invoked again"
  }
}
document.writeln(StaticTest.show());
</script>
```

A static method can also be invoked within a constructor. This is
demonstrated below:

```
<script>
class StaticTest {
  constructor() {
    document.writeln(StaticTest.show()+"<br>");
    document.writeln(this.constructor.show());
  }
```

```
    static show() {

        return "Static method has been invoked"

    }

}

var st=new StaticTest();
```
</script>

The code returns the following result:

Static method has been invoked
Static method has been invoked

A static method can also be invoked from within a non-static method.

For example:

<script>
```
class StaticTest {

    static show() {

        return "static method has been invoked"

    }

    show() {

        document.writeln(StaticTest.show()+"<br>");

    }

}

var st=new StaticTest();
st.show();
```

```
</script>
```

The code returns the following result:

static method has been invoked

Encapsulation

Encapsulation refers to the process of binding data together with the functions that act on that data. It is a good way of controlling data and validating it.

To achieve this in JavaScript, you should make the data members private using the *var* keyword. Setter methods can be used for setting the data while getter methods can be used for getting the data.

Consider the following example:

```
class Student
  {
    constructor()
    {
      var name;
      var score;
    }
      getStudentName()
      {
```

```
        return this.name;

      }

    setStudentName(name)

    {

      this.name=name;

    }

    getScore()

    {

      return this.score;

    }

  setScore(score)

  {

    this.score=score;

  }

  }

  var st=new Student();

    st.setStudentName("John");

    st.setScore(78);

    document.writeln(st.getStudentName()+"
"+st.getScore());
</script>
```

The code will return the following result after execution:

John 78

Let us see how we can validate the student's score:

```
<script>
class Student
  {
    constructor()
    {
       var name;
       var score;
    }
       getStudentName()
         {
            return this.name;
         }
       setStudentName(name)
       {
         this.name=name;
       }
       getScore()
       {
         return this.score;
       }
    setScore(score)
    {
        if(score<0||score>100)
```

```
        {
           alert("Invalid Score");
        }
     else
        {
           this.score=score;
        }
     }
   }
   var st=new Student();
    st.setStudentName("John");
    st.setScore(105);//alert() invokes
    document.writeln(st.getStudentName()+"
"+st.getScore());
</script>
```

The score has been validated in the ***setScore()*** method. If it is not between 0 and 100, it will be an invalid score. We have set the score to **105**. Execution of the code returns the following result:

Invalid Score

OK

Let us modify the score and set it to **78**:

```
<script>
class Student
  {
    constructor()
    {
       var name;
       var score;
    }
       getStudentName()
         {
            return this.name;
         }
       setStudentName(name)
       {
          this.name=name;
       }
       getScore()
       {
          return this.score;
       }
    setScore(score)
    {
        if(score<0||score>100)
```

```
            {
               alert("Invalid Score");
            }
         else
            {
               this.score=score;
            }
      }
      }
   var st=new Student();
     st.setStudentName("John");
     st.setScore(78);//alert() invokes
     document.writeln(st.getStudentName()+"
"+st.getScore());
</script>
```

The code returns the following result after execution:

```
John 78
```

We can also implement encapsulation using a prototype-based approach as shown below:

```
<script>
function Student(name,score)
{
  var sname=name;
```

```
var s_score=score;
Object.defineProperty(this,"name",{
  get:function()
  {
    return sname;
  },
set:function(sname)
{
  this.sname=sname;
}

});
    Object.defineProperty(this,"score",{
    get:function()
    {
      return s_score;
    },
  set:function(s_score)
  {
    this.s_score=s_score;
  }

});

}
```

```
  var st=new Student("John",78);
  document.writeln(st.name+" "+st.score);
</script>
```

The code will print the following output:

 John 78

Inheritance

With this JavaScript feature, we can create new classes that are based on the already existing classes. It provides a child class with a way to use the methods and properties that belong to the parent class.

In JavaScript, inheritance is done using the ***extends*** keyword. With this keyword, we create a child class that is based on the parent class. After that, the child class will be able to acquire the behavior and properties of the parent class.

Inheritance maintains the IS-A relationship. Inheritance can also be achieved using a prototype-based approach. Consider the following example where ***Current*** inherits ***Date***:

```
<script>
class Current extends Date {
  constructor() {
    super();
```

```
    }}
var c=new Current();
document.writeln("Today is on:")
document.writeln(c.getDate()+"-
"+(c.getMonth()+1)+"-"+c.getFullYear());
</script>
```

The code will return the output shown below:

Today is on: 20-2-2019

The code returns the date of today.

Here is another example:

```
<script>
class Current extends Date {
  constructor(year) {
    super(year);
  }}
var c=new Current("April 20, 1958 19:17:32");
document.writeln("The year is:")
document.writeln(c.getFullYear());
</script>
```

In the above example, we have created a date value and we have used the **getFullyear()** method to get the year only.

The code returns the following after execution:

The year is: 1958

This shows that the method was able to successfully extract only the year part of the provided date.

Here is another example in which we are creating a sub-class to inherit from the parent class:

```
<script>
class Car
{
  constructor()
  {
    this.manufacturer="Toyota";
  }
}
class Model extends Car {
  constructor(name,year) {
    super();
    this.name=name;
    this.year=year;
  }
}
var m = new Model("Harrier","2012");
```

```
document.writeln(m.manufacturer+" "+m.name+"
"+m.year);
</script>
```

The code returns the following result:

Toyota Harrier 2012

Let us demonstrate how prototype-based inheritance can be done, where we don't have to use the ***extends*** and ***class*** keywords:

```
<script>
 //A Constructor function
function Car(manufacturer)
{
    this.manufacturer=manufacturer;
}


Car.prototype.getManufacturer=function()
{
  return this.manufacturer;
}
//Another constructor function
//Second constructor function
function Model(name,year) {
 this.name=name;
    this.year=year;
```

```
      }
var car = new Car("Toyota");
model.prototype=car; //Now Bike treats as a
parent of Vehicle.
var model=new Model("Harrier",2012);
document.writeln(model.getManufacturer()+"
"+model.name+" "+model.year);
</script>
```

Polymorphism

This is a key feature of an object-oriented programming paradigm that makes it possible for one to perform a single action in different ways. With polymorphism, we can invoke one method on various JavaScript objects. JavaScript isn't a type-safe language; hence members of any data type can be passed with the methods. Consider the example given below:

```
<script>
class Parent
   {
      show()
      {
        document.writeln("Parent class invoked");
      }
   }
```

```
class Child extends Parent
    {
    }
var ch=new Child();
ch.show();
</script>
```

The code will return the following:

Parent class invoked

Here is another example:

```
<script>
class Parent
    {
       show()
        {
          document.writeln("Parent class
invoked<br>");
        }
    }
class Child extends Parent
    {
       show()
        {
          document.writeln("Child class invoked");
```

```
        }
     }
var p=[new Parent(), new Child()]
p.forEach(function(message)
{
message.show();
});
```

The ***show()*** method behaves differently based on the object for which it is invoked. The code prints the following output:

```
Parent class invoked
Child class invoked
```

We can implement the same example but this time via a prototype-based approach. This is demonstrated below:

```
<script>
function Parent()
{
}
Parent.prototype.show=function()
{
   return "Parent class invoked";
}
function Child()
{
```

```
}
Child.prototype=Object.create(Parent.prototype);
var p=[new Parent(), new Child()]
p.forEach(function(message)
{
  document.writeln(message.show()+"<br>");
});
<script>
```

Chapter 15- Multimedia

JavaScript has the ***plugin's*** object which is a child of ***navigator*** object. It's an array, and it comes with some single entry for a browser plugin. Browsers such as firefox and Netscape support the use of the ***navigator.plugins*** object.

 Consider the script given below:

```
< table border="1">

        <tr>
            <th> Name of PLugin</th>
            <th>Filename</th>
            <th>Description</th>
    </tr>
    <script language="JavaScript"
type="text/javascript">
        for (x= ; x<navigator.plugins.length;
x++) {
        document.write("<tr><td>");

document.write(navigator.plugins[x].name);
        document.write("</td><td>");
```

```
document.write(navigator.plugins[x].filename);
        document.write("</td><td>");

document.write(navigator.plugins[x].description)
;
        document.write("</td></tr>");
            }
        </script>
        </table>
```

Once executed, the script will show you a list of all plug-ins installed on your browser. Each plugin-in is represented as an entry in the array. Each entry has the following properties:

1. **name**- this specifies the name of a plugin.
2. **filename**- this is an executable file which is loaded in order to install a plugin.
3. **description**- this describes the plugin.

In my case, I ran the code on Chrome and it returned the following:

Name of PLugin	Filename	Description
Chrome PDF Viewer	mhjfbmdgcfjbbpaeojofohoefgiehjai	
Shockwave Flash	internal-not-yet-present	Shockwave Flash 21.0 r0
Chrome PDF Viewer	internal-pdf-viewer	Portable Document Format

With the above properties, one can determine the plugins which have been installed then use JavaScript so as to play the necessary multimedia file.

Example:

```
<script language="JavaScript"
type="text/javascript">
        vid =
navigator.mimeTypes["video/quicktime"];
        if (vid){
            document.write("<embed
src='movie1.mov'
            height=110 width=110>");
        }
        else
        {
            document.write("<img src='img1.gif'
            height=110 width=110>");
        }
    </script>
```

The **<embed>** tag has helped us to embed some multimedia file.

With JavaScript, we are able to control multimedia.

Example:

```
<       script type="text/javascript">

            function playMedia()
            {
               if (!document.game.IsPlaying()){
                  document.game.Play();
               }
            }
            function stopMedia()
            {
               if (document.game.IsPlaying()){
                  document.game.StopPlay();
               }
            }
            function rewindMedia()
            {
               if (document.game.IsPlaying()){
                  document.game.StopPlay();
               }
               document.game.Rewind();
            }
      </script>
   </head>
```

```
<body>

    <embed id="game" name="game"
    src="your_game_url"
    width="320" height="302" play="false"
loop="false"

pluginspage="http://www.macromedia.com/go/getfla
shplayer"
    swliveconnect="true">
    </embed>

    <form name="form1" id="form1" action="#"
method="get">
        <input type="button" value="Play"
onclick="playMedia();" />
        <input type="button" value="Stop"
onclick="stopMedia();" />
        <input type="button" value="Rewind"
onclick="rewindMedia();" />
    </form>
```

Ensure that you add the URL to the location of your game. Execute the script and you will see the buttons for Play, Stop and Rewind.

The example is capable of working on any browser.

Chapter 16- Error Handling

JavaScript is one of the loosely-typed languages that we have. It doesn't have a compile time. Errors normally occur during programming. You can attempt to access an undefined variable or function. The errors are classified as syntax errors, runtime errors and logical errors. Let us discuss them.

Syntax Errors

In JavaScript, syntax errors occur during interpret time. They are also known as *parsing errors.* Consider the sample script given below:

```
<script type="text/javascript">
      window.print()
</script>
```

JavaScript statement should end with a semicolon.

The **"window.print()"** statement doesn't end with a semicolon, hence this will result in a syntax error. If a statement has a syntax error, all statements in the same thread as this will be affected. The other threads will be executed normally.

Runtime Errors

These are the exceptions raised during runtime. Execution occurs after interpretation.

Example:

```
<script type="text/javascript">
        window.printFile();
</script>
```

During interpretation, no error will be raised since the script has the correct syntax. However, an exception will be raised during runtime as the script will call a method which is unknown, that is, the ***printFile()*** method.

Logical Errors

These types of errors occur when you fail to implement the right logic in your script, meaning you will not get the expected results. They can be hard for one to track. They don't result from either runtime or syntax errors. One cannot catch those types of errors since they depend on the business logic to be implemented.

try...catch...finally

With JavaScript, you can handle errors and exceptions. When this statement is combined with the *throw*, one can handle errors and exceptions more effectively. The statement has the syntax given below:

```
< script type="text/javascript">

    try {
        // your code
        [break;]
    }
    catch ( ex ) {
        // code to execute in case of exception
        [break;]
    }
    [ finally {
        // Code to execute whether the
exception occurs or not.
    }]
</script>
```

A try block should be followed by either catch or *finally* block. On the occurrence of the exception in try block, an exception will be added to the ex, then catch block will be executed. The *final* block is optional and it is unconditionally executed after the **try/catch**. Example:

```
<script>
function checkFunction() {
```

```javascript
    var check, val;
    check = document.getElementById("check");
    check.innerHTML = "";
    val =
document.getElementById("field").value;
    try {
        if(val == "")   throw "empty";
        if(isNaN(val)) throw "Enter a number";
        val = Number(val);
        if(val < 10)     throw "too low";
        if(val > 20)     throw "too high";
    }
    catch(ex) {
        check.innerHTML = "Your input is " + ex;
    }
}
</script>
```

In our case, we are using the try and catch to validate our input field. The input should be a number ranging between 10 and 20. If this is not adhered to, an exception will be raised then handled by the try and catch.

finally Statement

This statement specifies the code to be executed after a try and catch, and it must be executed regardless of the result. The following is its syntax:

```
try {
    Code for try
}
catch(err) {
    code for handling errors
}
finally {
    code for finally
}
```

Example:

```
< script>

function checkFunction() {
    var check, val;
    check = document.getElementById("check");
    check.innerHTML = "";
    val =
document.getElementById("field").value;
    try {
        if(val == "")   throw "It is empty";
```

```
        if(isNaN(val)) throw "Enter a number";

        val = Number(val);

        if(val > 20)    throw "number too high";

        if(val < 10)     throw "number too low";

   }
   catch(ex) {

        check.innerHTML = "Input " + ex;

   }
   finally {

        document.getElementById("field").value =
"";

   }
}
```
```
</script>
```

The field value will cleared, which is implemented in the *finally* block.

Chapter 17- Regular Expressions

A regular expression refers to a pattern created by characters. JavaScript has a class named **RegExp** which helps programmers work with regular expressions. With this class, one can perform pattern matching, replace and search functions on some text.

To define a regular expression, we use the **RegExp()** constructor. This is demonstrated below:

```
regexpression = new RegExp("the_pattern",
"flags");
```

The parameter **the_pattern** is a string specifying the pattern of regular expression or any other regular expression. The **flags** parameter is an optional string with either the **"i"**, **"m"** and **"g"** attributes specifying case-insensitive, multi-line and global matches respectively.

Let us discuss the various methods for Regular Expressions in JavaScript.

exec()

This method will search a string for text matching the regexp. If a match is found, the results will be returned in an array, otherwise, it will return null.

The method has the following syntax:

```
RegExpObject.exec( search_string );
```

The parameter ***search_string*** denotes the string that is to be searched for.

Consider the following example:

```
<script type = "text/javascript">
        var text = "JavaScript has a class
named RegExp which helps programmers work with
regular expressions";
        var reg = new RegExp( "express", "g" );

        var output = reg.exec(text);
        document.write("First test, the
returned value is: " +  output);

        reg = new RegExp( "language", "g" );

        var output = reg.exec(text);
        document.write("<br />Second test, the
returned value is: " +  output);
    </script>
```

The code returns the following output after execution:

```
First test, the returned value is: express
Second test, the returned value is: null
```

We first searched for the string *express* which was found in the **expressions**. Secondly, we searched for the string **language** and it was not found in our sentence.

test()

This method searches a string for text matching the regexp. If a match is found, it will return a **true**, otherwise, it will return a **false**. The method has the syntax given below:

```
RegExpObject.test( search_string );
```

The *search_string* is the string that is to be searched.

Consider the following example:

```
<script type = "text/javascript">

        var text = "JavaScript has a class
named RegExp which helps programmers work with
regular expressions";
        var reg = new RegExp( "express", "g" );

        var output = reg.test(text);
```

```
        document.write("First test returned: "
+   output);

        reg = new RegExp( "language", "g" );

        var output = reg.test(text);
        document.write("<br />Second test
returned: " +   output);
    </script>
```

The code returns the following result:

First test returned: true
Second test returned: false

In the first test, a match was found, hence the output is *true*. In the second test, no match was found, hence it returned a *false*.

search()

This method searches for a string, similarly to *indexOf()* function except that it will take a regular exception rather than a string. An integer is returned indicating the string position. Note that **o** indicates the beginning of a string, **7** will match the **8th** character, etc. If no match is found, then a **-1** will be returned:

```
<script type = "text/javascript">
    var myString = "best1 Best2 BEST3";
```

```
var m= myString.search(/Best[0-9]+/);
document.writeln(m)
</script>
```

The scripts returns a **6** upon execution.

toString()

When used, this method will return the string representation of the regular expression in question in regular expression literal form. The method takes the syntax given below:

```
RegExpObject.toString();
```

The method then returns a string representation of your regular expression.

For example:

```
<script type = "text/javascript">
    var text = "JavaScript has a class named
RegExp which helps programmers work with regular
expressions";
var reg = new RegExp( "express", "g" );
        var output = reg.toString(text);
        document.write("First test returned: "
+  output);
        reg = new RegExp( "/", "g"
        var output = reg.toString(text);
```

```
        document.write("<br />Second test
returned: " +  output);
    </script>
```

The code will return the following result upon execution:

First test returned: /express/g
Second test returned: /V/g

Chapter 18- Image Map

JavaScript can be used for the creation of a client side image map. To enable client-side image maps, we use the ***usemap*** attribute of **<img />** tag. We use the **<area>** and **<map>** extension tags to define them. The image to form the map is inserted using the **<img />** tag and a special attribute known as ***usemap***. The value for this attribute should match the value of the ***name*** attribute used in the **<map>** element, and it should be preceded by a hash or pound sign.

The **<map>** tag creates a map for your image and it should come after the **<img />** element. It will form the container for **<area />** elements defining the clickable hotspots. The **<map>** element has only one attribute, ***name*** attribute, which is a name identifying the map. This helps the **<img />** element know the **<map>** element which it is to use.

The coordinates and the shape of the clickable hotspots are defined using the **<area>** element. Consider the following example:

```
<html>
    <head>
        <script type = "text/javascript">
            <!--
```

```
        function showLanguage(name) {
            document.form1.lang.value = name
        }
    //-->
    </script>
  </head>
  <body>
    <form name = "form1">
        <input type = "text" name = "lang" size
= "20" />
    </form>
    <img src = "/images/usemap.gif" alt =
"Languages" border = "0" usemap = "#languages"/>
    <map name = "languages">
        <area shape="poly"
            coords =
"74,0,113,29,98,72,52,72,38,27"
            href = "perl.htm" alt = "Perl"
            target = "_self"
            onMouseOver = "showLanguage('Perl')"
            onMouseOut = "showLanguage('')"/>

        <area shape = "rect"
            coords = "22,83,126,125"
            href = "/html.org" alt = "Html"
```

```
            target = "_self"
            onMouseOver = "showLanguage('Html')"
            onMouseOut = "showLanguage('')"/>


        <area shape = "circle"
            coords = "73,168,32"
            href = "/php.org" alt = "Php"
            target = "_self"
            onMouseOver = "showLanguage('Php')"
            onMouseOut = "showLanguage('')"/>
        </map>
    </body>
</html>
```

The code gives me an interface after execution. The result I get on the input field depends on the part I point at as shown below:

Chapter 19- Page Redirection

Sometimes, you encounter situations in which you click on a **URL** to visit a certain page **X** but you are internally directed to another page **Y**. This is how *page redirection* works.

There are a number of reasons as to why you may need to redirect your users to another page. A good example is when you move to a new domain. You can use page redirection to direct your visitors to the new website. In such a case, you only have to maintain your old domain then add a single page with the page redirection feature so that anyone who visits your old domain is taken to your new website.

Sometimes, you can create different web pages for different versions of browsers or when the pages are for different countries. Instead of relying on server side page redirection, you can choose to use client side page redirection to ensure that each visits lands on the right page.

Page redirection is also important in cases where your web pages have been indexed by the search engines. When you move to a new domain, there is no need for you to lose your search engine visitors. In this case, the client side page redirection will help you. However, don't do it as a way of fooling the browsers as doing so may see your web pages banned on the browsers.

Client side page redirection can be implemented easily in JavaScript. To do this, you are only required to add a line at the head section of your code. This will do the redirection. Let us demonstrate this:

```html
<html>
   <head>
       <script type="text/javascript">
          <!--
            function RedirectFunction() {

window.location="https://www.javascript.com";
             }
          //-->
       </script>

   </head>

   <body>
       <p> Click the button given below for
redirection </p>

       <form>
          <input type="button" value="Redirect"
onclick="RedirectFunction();" />
```

```
        </form>
    </body>
</html>
```

The code will return the following upon execution:

Click the button given below for redirection

Redirect

Click the Redirect button and see what happens. You should be redirected to the URL that you have specified. In the above case, I have specified JavaScript website as the URL. You can change and see it redirect you to another website.

It is possible for you to display a message to the visitors before you can redirect them to a new page. However, a bit of delay will be needed for the new page to be loaded. Let us demonstrate how this can be implemented:

```
<html>
    <head>

        <script type="text/javascript">
            function RedirectFunction() {

window.location="https://www.javascript.com";
            }
```

```
        document.write("You will see the
main page in 10 seconds.");
        setTimeout('RedirectFunction()',
10000);
    </script>

</head>

<body>
</body>
</html>
```

After running the code, you will see the following message:

You will see the main page in 10 seconds.

After the expiry of the 10 seconds, you will be redirected to the JavaScript website.

As we had stated earlier, page redirection can be done based on the browser of the user. The following example demonstrates how this can be done:

```
<html>
    <head>
        <script type = "text/javascript">
```

```
        <!--
          var browsertype = navigator.appName;
          if( browsertype == "Netscape" ) {
             window.location =
"http://www.netscape.com";
          } else if ( browsertype =="Microsoft
Internet Explorer") {
                window.location =
"http://www.microsoft.com";
          } else {
              window.location =
"http://www.javascript.com";
          }
          //-->
      </script>
    </head>

    <body>
    </body>
</html>
```

The user will then be redirected based on the type of browser they are using. Note that we have used decision making statement *if* to redirect the users to different pages.

Conclusion

This marks the end of this guide. JavaScript is a very powerful scripting language. JavaScript is an interpreted scripting language. The language is normally executed on the client side. This makes it the best language for validations during web development. Web developers use JavaScript to validate their web forms for valid email addresses, phone numbers, and other details. JavaScript has changed the way things are done. Initially, after filling a form, one had to submit it to the server so that it could be checked for any anomalies. If anomalies were found, the server would return the form to the user in order to correct the details. The user would then re-submit the details filled in the form. With JavaScript, validation is done before the form can be submitted to the server. The user is able to know any errors done while filling the form and correct them accordingly. This has made things easy for users. JavaScript also allows you to create various effects that can be invoked by some of your actions. Examples of these actions can be a hover of the mouse cursor, a press of a keyboard key, loading of a web page, etc.

www.ingramcontent.com/pod-product-compliance
Lightning Source LLC
Chambersburg PA
CBHW071418050326
40689CB00010B/1891